Coping with Christmas

PETER COREY

illustrated by
mike phillips

Hippo

Scholastic Children's Books
Commonwealth House, 1-19 New Oxford Street
London WC1A 1NU, UK

a division of Scholastic Ltd
London ~ New York ~ Toronto ~ Sydney ~ Auckland
Mexico City ~ New Delhi ~ Hong Kong

First published in the UK by Scholastic Ltd, 1999

Text copyright © Peter Corey, 1999
Cover illustration copyright © Philip Reeve, 1999
Inside illustrations copyright © Mike Phillips, 1999

ISBN 0 439 01187 6

Typeset by TW Typesetting, Midsomer Norton, Somerset
Printed by Cox & Wyman Ltd, Reading, Berks.

10 9 8 7 6 5 4 3 2 1

The right of Peter Corey, Philip Reeve and Mike Phillips to be identified as
the author and illustrators of this work respectively has been asserted by
them in accordance with the Copyright, Designs and Patents Act, 1988.

Contents

Dedication:

This book is dedicated to Joel, Hannah, James, Megan and Jack, who never fail to realize that Christmas is for kids - kids like me.

It is also dedicated to all my relatives, who thankfully have come to realize that Christmas does *not* mean socks!

Dear new book owner

Well, it's Christmas again and hopefully all that being nice, keeping your room tidy or continual nagging has paid off and you've got what you wanted. Maybe this book was in among the stuff that you...

The stuff that frankly either fills you with delight or horror; the kind of stuff that comes from relatives; stuff that might be safer plunged into a bucket of water rather than opened. If this was just such a gift I hope you didn't plunge it into a bucket of water, because, despite many requests from me, Scholastic have not yet seen the wisdom of making my books waterproof.

Whatever situation has led to you being the owner of this book – READ IT NOW, because this is a book about surviving Christmas. If you read it *after* Christmas, you'll only find yourself going: "Oh no! If only I'd read this book sooner I could have avoided such-and-such a situation". So take yourself off to a large cupboard with a torch, a reasonable amount of Christmas food and drink and start reading. Believe me you'll be really glad you did.

IF YOU ARE STANDING IN A SHOP LOOKING AT THIS BOOK, THEN SEE OVER THE PAGE...

Dear potential book owner

Hello. So here you are then. Trying to decide what to buy your girl/boyfriend for Christmas, and asking yourself some or all of the following questions:

1. If I buy her/him a Christmas present, will they think I'm being flash and dump me?

2. If I *don't* buy them a present will they think I'm being mean and dump me?

3. Will they dump me anyway?

Or maybe it's after Christmas and you're trying to decide how to dispose of that book token your Auntie Brenda gave you. When will that woman realize that you'd rather have the money? Do you ever give *her* a book token? Of course not! Do you ever give her *anything*? Well, no, but surely that's not the point. The point is that money is much more useful than a book token. Not that there's anything wrong with books; books are *cool*. I should know, I write them. I even read one once; it was green. No – books are fine.

But *money* – now there's a really useful commodity. You can buy stuff with money; stuff like books.

Anyway here you are, clutching your book token and wondering how on earth you got through Christmas. More to the point, how are you going to get through *next* year? I can't answer the first question, but the second one's simple – with the help of this book. Because this book contains all you'll ever need to know about the so-called festive season, and a few things that you'd probably rather not be reminded about. All you need to do is buy it. So forget that copy of *Plumbing Can Be Fun* by H and C Runningwater,[1] even if it has got a rather nice sketch of a tap on the cover. This is the book for you.

1: The finest Native American plumbers this side of the Colorado desert. Not only can they fix the central heating but they can also get the tap working just by doing a little dance.

8

So whether you got the book as a present, or you've just bought it for yourself, you can now relax. I am here. I will guide you gently through the horrific minefield that can be Christmas. And I'll start right now - just on the next page.

Christmas - what is it?

As any regular reader of my books will know, I am a firm believer in the fact that, in order to be able to cope with something, you have to know exactly what it is you're faced with. So what exactly *is* Christmas? Or to put it another way: what exactly *was* Christmas? Or to put it even another way: mndw gvqw dkj yvtw e faweu yfvil? No I think the second way is best: what exactly *was* Christmas? To discover that we need to go back about 2,000 years to the little town of Bethlehem in the kingdom of Judea.

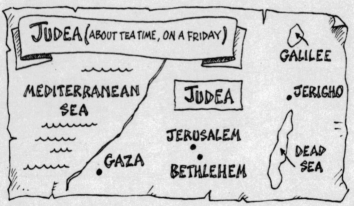

JUDEA (ABOUT TEA TIME, ON A FRIDAY)

GALILEE

MEDITERRANEAN SEA

JUDEA

JERICHO

JERUSALEM

GAZA

BETHLEHEM

DEAD SEA

In the beginning...

It isn't easy being a shepherd. What with BSE, scrapie and *Emmerdale*.[1] And that's just these days. Imagine what it was like in … ah. Our first problem. What year was it? Of course we now know it as AD 1,[2] but it wasn't called that then. In fact, what year it was rather

1: If you're reading this book in Australia or on the planet Urff, I should point out that *Emmerdale* is a popular UK "soap", a bit like *Neighbours* with cows.

2: AD is short for Anno Domini – which is Latin for in "the Year of Our Lord".

depended on where you lived. The Jewish calendar reckoned it was the year 3760. Our shepherd, sitting there on the hill overlooking Bethlehem was probably Jewish, even though his name was Colin. The Romans reckoned it was 753, and since the Romans were currently in charge you dared not argue with them. The Egyptians, who used to be in charge before Moses led the Jews out of slavery, made it the year 4236; Colin's mate Eric, who was Babylonian, swore blind that it was 749. But then Eric swore about most things – the cold, the wet, the price of sheep dip – everything. No, it wasn't easy being a shepherd.

And it *was* cold. It was a "bleak mid-winter", according to the well-known carol. "Frosty winds made moan," she says. The shepherds were just wondering whether or not it was too cold to "wash their socks by night", which was a local custom in those days, underwear being something that you didn't really flash around in public, when "the Angel of the Lord came down and glory shone around".

"Fear not," said the angel. Well frankly, that was easy for him to say. He was an angel, he lived at God's right hand and so he was probably used to seeing all sorts of strange manifestations. But the shepherds weren't.

Frankly, the scariest thing Colin had ever seen was a follower of the One God being dangled upside down into a pit of killer gerbils. The Romans were big on that sort of thing. They couldn't quite buy the idea of there only being one God. After all, the Romans had gods for everything: war, rain, love, those little rough bits that you get on the side of your fingernail if you accidentally catch it on your toga – everything. So they really couldn't see the point of only having one God. What's more, the Jews couldn't even tell you what he looked liked or where He lived.

The idea of One God is not as straightforward as it may seem.

Nevertheless, if the Romans had read their scripture (which, of course, being Romans and not Jews, they weren't interested in), they might have been a little more nervous about this One God the Jews had. After all, look what happened in Egypt. Moses had said to the Pharaoh "let my people go," to which the Pharaoh said "no". So what happened? God stepped in, apparently. After plagues of boils, blood, frogs, deaths of the first born, scattered showers and a rather unpleasant north-easterly breeze with a bit of a chill factor, Pharaoh was begging them to leave and even laying on transport. This Jewish God was obviously not somebody to mess with, though the Romans didn't know it.

One thing the Jews knew for sure was that the prophets had foretold that one day – probably a Thursday – God would send His only Son to save the world.

"What from?"

"The Romans, probably. Or Cliff Richard."

So to cut a long story short, when the Angel of the Lord told the shepherds that the Son of God had been born in Bethlehem, they were down that hill quicker than you could say, "Will somebody look after these sheep for half an hour while I nip into town, please?"

Bethlehem was particularly crowded that winter. The Romans had ordered a census, which is a Latin word meaning … er … census. They wanted to count everyone up to work out how much they should be getting in taxes.

For the census the Romans told everybody to return to the place where they had been born. This immediately caused problems. Every day the Roman civil service were fielding enquiries from people saying things like: "How can I return to the place where I was born? You lot have knocked it down and built an aqueduct!" Anyway, because of the census the town was packed. People had come from miles around.

People, in many cases, who had been glad to see the back of the place when they had originally left it. After all, Bethlehem was a bit of a one-horse town – or one-donkey town to be more exact. Little did any of them realize that events of that night would put the town firmly on the map for ever.

But how was that going to happen? Well, it had quite a lot to do with a young couple. They had travelled from Nazareth in Galilee, about 80 miles from Bethlehem. That must seem a very long way indeed when riding on a donkey, particularly if one of you is pregnant, which the young woman was.

Getting hotel accommodation in those days was a lot trickier than it is now. You couldn't phone ahead and book, confirming by fax and securing your room with a credit card. You just had to turn up and hope for the best. If you were lucky you got a room with en suite facilities and the promise of a TV as soon as somebody invents one; if you weren't, you didn't. The young couple weren't. And so it was that they found themselves sleeping in a stable.

THE HAY GETS CHANGED TUESDAYS AND THURSDAYS, THERE'S HOT AND COLD RUNNING SHEEP AND A PARKING SPACE FOR YOUR DONKEY

Their names were Mary and Joseph, and later that same evening, the baby was born.

And it was in this stable that Colin and the other shepherds eventually found Mary, Joseph and their new baby, whose name was Jesus.

Despite the surroundings you could tell that the child was special. He had a sort of aura about him. He wasn't like other babies.

"He ain't like your Cheryl's Wayne. When he was born he looked like a septic boil," said Eric, who was taking Romantic Poetry lessons one day a week at Bethlehem Tech.

Colin and his mates were not the only visitors.

Somewhere in the east three wise astrologers were passing the time by doing each other's horoscopes.

"You're about to go on a long journey," said one of them, as he studied a hastily drawn star chart.

"Not in this weather I'm not!" retorted his colleague.

Just then there was a knock on the door.

"A customer!" exclaimed astrologer number three, wiping his hands on his mystic robes. He had been peeling potatoes for a hot-pot, a favourite dish among wise men everywhere.

A bright light shone through the cracks of the ill-fitting door.

"Let him in and ask him where he bought his torch. I could do with one as bright as that if I'm going on a long journey."

The moment the door opened they realized that this was no ordinary "punter". They listened carefully to what he had to say. They were indeed going on a long journey.

In those days it was customary to take gifts with you if you were going visiting. This was partly to repay your host for their hospitality, and partly to have something to bribe any would-be robbers who fancied slitting your throat. Because of this, our three wise men were able to present the new-born baby with expensive gifts of gold, frankincense and myrrh. The shepherds brought a sheep; being a shepherd wasn't as well paid as astrology.

THESE ARE VERY NICE, BUT DIDN'T ANYONE BRING A TEDDY OR A RATTLE?

And so it was that, while the hotels of Bethlehem took advantage of their late-night licences to make a real financial killing, a child was born who would change the world. He would be called Christ – the Son of God – and His birthday would be called Christmas.

But not in His lifetime. In fact, Christmas didn't happen for another 350 years or more. Why not?

Because although many people agreed that Jesus was a wonderful person,[1] some of them found His claim to be the Son of God a bit much to take – blasphemous even.

Oh yes, the scriptures had predicted that God would send his Son into the world, but most of the learned scribes and holy men were pretty certain that it wouldn't happen this way.

"After all," they argued, "A God who can part seas and send plagues of frogs isn't going to allow His Son to be born in a stable, to some young couple that nobody's ever heard of who aren't even technically *married*! It's ridiculous!"

Those people who believed that Jesus *was* the Son of God became known as Christians, and despite years of persecution their belief spread until it became the major religion of the Western world.

Even the Romans, who had done more than most to stamp out Christianity, were eventually converted.

1: Not the Romans, though, who thought he was a tricky customer and allowed Him to be put to death.

17

It was the Roman Pope Gregory who decided that Jesus' birthday would be celebrated on 25 December. He made this decision in a year that eventually became known as AD 354. The big question is...

Why the 25th?

Having been converted, the Romans were probably keen to stamp out festivals that related to other gods. The big winter one was Saturnalia, the festival of Saturn, god of the Harvest. This was on 19 December and lasted for a week. It involved a lot of partying – something the Romans were famous for. Ironically, it also involved a lot of throwing Christians to lions, something else the Romans were particularly good at. Until they became Christians themselves, then they went right off it.

25 December was actually a good date to pick, because it coincided with at least two other "pagan"[1] festivals: the winter solstice which celebrated the coming of Spring; and Yule – a north European festival which involved setting fire to logs decorated with greenery and ribbons. The idea behind this one was to encourage the Nordic gods to make the sun shine a bit

1: I.e. non-Christian.

more. Which, when you consider that Sweden only has a few hours of daylight in the winter, is not a bad idea!

The Nativity crib and the singing of carols were added in the Middle Ages, by which time Christmas had become a 12 day celebration – not to mention a massive eating competition, with meals lasting about nine hours at a time!

This went on until 1652, when the Puritans banned the Christmas festivities, particularly the pudding, which gave them wind.

Although Christmas was revived in 1660, just in time for the Great Fire of London, many of the things like Yule logs and carols weren't revived until Victorian times.

Queen Victoria's husband, Prince Albert, introduced the Christmas tree to this country, although they'd had them in Germany for centuries.

Christmas cards first came about in 1846 in London, although they didn't really catch on until the 1870s. This was probably because the post was very slow in those days.

Christmas crackers were invented in the late nineteenth century by an English baker called Tom Smith. By 1900 he was selling 3,000 of them worldwide! But what about Santa Claus? Well, the bloke on the sleigh with reindeers and a sack of toys was invented by the Americans. He first appeared in *Harper's Magazine* in 1868.

But the *real* Father Christmas is descended from Saint Nicholas ("Santa Claus" is how people said "Saint Nicholas" when they'd had too much brandy in their Christmas pudding.) In Russia he is usually depicted with a piglet under his arm. An early example of a packed lunch.

A typical nineteenth-century Christmas might have panned out something like this:

24 DECEMBER: CHRISTMAS EVE

1. Light the candles on the Christmas tree.
2. Call the fire brigade (if you've overdone the candles).
3. Sing carols around the tree.
4. Exchange gifts.
5. Go to midnight mass.

25 DECEMBER: CHRISTMAS DAY

1. Eat
2. Eat
3. Eat
4. Be sick (optional)
5. Eat

26 DECEMBER: BOXING DAY

1. Give small gifts (Christmas "boxes") to your servants and the local tradesmen.
2. Feel very ill.

That's what *should* happen now. That's *traditional*. But as we all know, there's a lot more to Christmas than a simple religious festival. *Lots* more!

Religious note

Before we get into the nitty gritty of a modern Christmas, it's worth mentioning that not everybody celebrates Christmas. As I've already pointed out, Christmas is a Christian religious festival, originally celebrated by people who believed that Christ was the Son of God. But these days this doesn't necessarily stop other religions joining the party. They often use it more as a chance either to celebrate their own faith, or simply to bring the family together. Ironically it's this "bringing the family together" that can cause most of the problems – but more of that later.

The Americans get around the fact that Christmas is a Christian celebration and that they (like us) are a multi-cultural society, by calling Christmas *The Holidays*, which when you think about it can mean anything. Ironically, Christmas is anything *but* a holiday! But where does it all begin?

Pre-Christmas Panic

You can tell that Christmas is not far off when the high street shops start stocking Easter eggs. Christmas seems to start earlier and earlier each year. At least, it does for adults. I know a woman who starts stock-piling Christmas presents the minute she gets back from her summer holidays. In fact, some years she does it *instead of* going on holiday! All of her nooks, crannies, cupboards and even her drawers are crammed with would-be Christmas gifts. Of course, her kids *know* that she does this, and so every day is a treasure hunt. They've usually found the lot by the middle of October!

IF YOU KEEP GOING INTO THOSE CUPBOARDS, FATHER CHRISTMAS WON'T COME!

HE NEEDN'T BOTHER – I'LL HAVE THIS LOT INSTEAD!

Even in my house we try to spread the cost of Christmas by buying stamps from the milkman to pay for the food hamper. We religiously stick the stamps in a booklet and promptly lose it a week before we're due to make the exchange. By the time he arrives we're lucky if we can afford a Christmas *hamster*, let alone a hamper!

And that's another thing – pets for Christmas. Why is it that... Woah! Hang on! I'm doing it myself! I'm letting Christmas run away with me! One thing at a time. Let's start slowly at the beginning of Christmas, which if you're lucky is also the beginning of December.

GETTING THAT FESTIVE FEELING

December the first; 25 days to go until the big day. It seems almost a month away as you open the first little door on your Advent calendar.

Advent? What's all that about then?

Well, according to *The Bumper Book of Festive Stuff*, Advent is the name given to the four weeks before Christmas, starting on St. Andrew's Day (30 November) or the Sunday nearest to it. This Sunday was the day when traditionally the Christmas Pudding had to be mixed. It was put in a large bowl and each member of the family (including the dog, probably) had to have a go at stirring it anti-clockwise. Actually, maybe the dog didn't have a stir. After all, most dogs don't know their leg from a stick, so the chances of them knowing clockwise from anti-clockwise are non-existent. Some people say that you should stir from east to west, to emulate the journey of the Three Wise Men, so it's probably a good idea to use a spoon with a compass attached.

Anyway getting back to tradition, everybody else had a stir. The pudding was then boiled for about six hours, after which it was left to stand until Christmas day.

That explains the revolting taste, then.

Other Advent customs include hanging an Advent

wreath from the ceiling of the living room. The wreath is made of holly and ivy, and has four candles set into it. On each of the four Sundays of Advent, one of the candles is lit. On the final Sunday before Christmas the final candle is lit, the smoke alarms go off and the house burns down, causing the family to spend Christmas sleeping in an old barn, just like Jesus and His family had to all those years ago.

The word "Advent" comes from the Roman word *adventus*, meaning "arrival", which obviously refers to the arrival of Jesus. Roman Catholics are not allowed to get married during Advent. Not that they'd have much time to get married; they'd be far too busy standing under the Advent wreath holding a fire extinguisher.

Of course, to most of us Advent means a large calendar with 25 little doors in it. Behind each door there's a picture and a chocolate. At least, the instructions *say* that they're chocolates. Frankly if you found one lying on the carpet you'd think that your hamster had had an accident. Of course, the makers of these advent calendars would have you believe that these chocolates were specially hand-crafted to depict a typical Christmas scene. But the reason they put the little picture there as well is because without it you'd never work out what the chocolate was meant to depict.

But why bother with a chocolate anyway?

Surely the excitement of opening a little door every day, knowing that it was bringing Christmas 24 hours nearer should be enough. Well yes, it should; for anyone who doesn't get out much.

But the chocolate has another, possibly more sinister, purpose.

Everybody knows – or at least if you don't you're

about to – that chocolate contains caffeine. Caffeine is well-known, notorious even, for keeping you awake. So by giving you a small but highly concentrated dose of caffeine every day for 25 days the Advent calendar manufacturers are ensuring that:

A) YOU DON'T FALL ASLEEP IN THE MIDDLE OF CHRISTMAS DINNER (OR THE QUEEN'S SPEECH).

CHOCOLATE SAUCE...

B) YOU GET SO HYPERACTIVE BY CHRISTMAS DAY THAT YOU CAN'T *FAIL* TO THINK YOU'RE HAVING A GOOD TIME.

YAHOO!

If you need to be further convinced of this obvious truth, think about your parents/aunts/uncles/grannies etc. Do they have Advent calendars? No. Do they fall asleep/get grumpy over Christmas? Yes. I rest my case.

And so in the best traditions of Christmas, I have created within the pages of this wonderful book an Advent calendar for us to share; one that will help us through the dark and dreary days of Advent. It goes right up to the early hours of Christmas morning, when small children everywhere can be heard to say, "Has he been?" in wide-eyed wonderment; and you and I can be heard saying, "If it's socks again I'll kill them!" So step up to the mantelpiece with me, and help me prise back the little door on December the first.

ADVENT-COUNTDOWN TO DISAPPOINTMENT

I think we might need a crowbar. Why do they make these little doors so hard to open? After all, if the little door falls open by mistake, what do they imagine is going to happen? Are 24 hours suddenly going to be wiped off the Christmas countdown? I don't think so. If they were, of course, that would be a disaster. Santa's Elves would have to work overtime to get all the toys ready; the shops would lose huge amounts of money due to losing 24 hours of trading time; distant relatives would arrive sooner. This last thing would really be a disaster – but more about them later. By unwrapping Dad's present of a multi-purpose drill and Advent calendar opener,[1] we are able to get the door open to reveal...

What is it? Some sort of Christmas gift, I imagine. These are just the sort of gifts that you get at Christmas that make you go: "What is it?" because there's nothing about the shape that gives you any clue. Because of this, a simple square box can take on all sorts of mysterious properties. You become fascinated by it; you leave it until last, knowing deep down that it is *bound* to be something *amazing*, even though you've read the tag and know that it comes from your Auntie Doreen and her idea of amazing would be a set of matching socks and pants.

1: To which he will say: "Wow! Just what I always wanted!" But he says that every year. He even said it the year you gave him double pneumonia.

"Just imagine how impressed the hospital will be when they discover that your underwear is *co-ordinated*," she tells you, smugly.

"Hospital?" say you.

"Yes," says Auntie.

"Why would I want to go to hospital?" you ask, not really wanting to know.

"When you get run over," explains Auntie. "Christmas is a notoriously dangerous time to be out and about."

"Out and about? The furthest I'm likely to go this Christmas is down the garden to crack the ice on the water in the bird table."

This is just the sort of good deed you're famous for at Christmas – your kindness to dumb animals; you even talk to your younger *brother*, and if that's not an act of self-sacrifice I'd like to know what is! The local birds are always impressed and grateful; it doesn't stop them trying to dive-bomb you all year round, but they *are* grateful.

Anyway – where were we? Oh yes, presents. For most of us this is what Christmas is all about. Not just the receiving, although obviously that's the most important part; the giving is also quite crucial, not to say stressful. Somebody once said that it was better to give than to receive. They should have added that it's also a real pain.

I GAVE MY GIRLFRIEND ONE OF MY OLD JUMPERS FOR CHRISTMAS AND I RECEIVED A BLACK EYE!

Just think about it.

Every year you vow that you'll get some really nice presents for those few chosen friends and relatives that you want to impress; the ones who always put a lot of thought into your gift. Every year you say to yourself, "It doesn't need to be anything *big*. After all, it's the *thought* that counts." How right you are! Size isn't everything. Obviously it needs to be big enough for them to see; there's not a lot of point in carefully choosing a gift if your friend/relative accidentally throws it away with the wrapping paper. So you really make an effort and give it plenty of thought. So much so that you realize that if you put the same amount of thought into your homework you'd be the cleverest person in the school. But then why waste a precious thing like *thought* on school when you could save it for something really important, like Christmas presents?

But Christmas presents, no matter how much thought goes into them, have one huge drawback: they cost money.

And money – as we all know – is not easy to come by. It's terrible isn't it, but it just doesn't matter how hard you try, how much you resolve to put money by for those all-important Christmas presents, something always comes along and eats into your Christmas funds. You get a bit put by, and then Easter comes along. Well, you've got to buy an Easter egg, haven't you – just in case the one your parents get you isn't quite big enough. And then there's the summer holidays. By the time you've sent postcards to relatives who barely talk to you from one year to the next, and bought sticks of rock for every neighbour within a five-mile radius, your Christmas gift fund is down to a few pence.

Do you give up? Of course you don't! You offer to do jobs around the house in the hope of replenishing your cash stash. You clean Dad's car, and what happens? He gives you fifty pence! *FIFTY PENCE!*

Where has this man been for the past 20 years? Hasn't he heard of the minimum wage? Your average car takes about two hours to clean properly,[1] which means that he should be paying you … erm … lots more than fifty pence!

The trouble with parents is that they have absolutely no notion of what people should be paid. Would they work for fifty pence? Of course they wouldn't![2] So why should you? And then of course, there's specialized

1: OK, so it only normally takes you ten seconds to clean your parents' car – but that's only because you want to make sure that it gets dirty again in time for your next cash crisis, isn't it? Isn't it? Oh.
2: Unless of course they're a teacher or a nurse, but then they're a special case, apparently.

work which clearly should attract a higher rate of pay. I'm talking about stuff like tidying your room – if that doesn't require real specialist skill, I'd like to know what does.

DON'T WORRY, I'LL HAVE THIS DONE IN A JIFFY!

But I digress. The long and short of the situation is that whatever you do, however hard you try, you are going to go into this Christmas Countdown period seriously short of cash and wondering how on Earth you're going to afford any presents.

So what can you do?

Obviously you will have made a list of all the people you feel you *ought* to be buying for. Well, you can cross off any brothers or sisters for a start. Let's face it, you don't like them, they don't like you, and Christmas really isn't likely to alter that. Besides the Christmas message is "good will to all *men*"; it doesn't say anything about brothers or sisters.[1]

You can also cross off any ex-boy/girlfriends, unless there's a serious chance of getting back together again. Even if there is, you can always use an unwanted gift token to get them something *after* Christmas. A late

1: Come to think of it, it doesn't specifically mention mums, dads or any relatives either.

gift can be quite romantic - as long as it's only *days* late and not *years*.

So by now you've whittled the list down to your mum and dad and a few odd relatives. Cross off the relatives, unless they're coming to stay. No - cross them off anyway. If they look disappointed about not getting a gift from you, you can always say, "I didn't get you a gift because I thought you were dead." OK, so it's not the subtlest thing to say, but if it's said with a cheery smile and quickly followed with a heartfelt, "I'm really pleased you're not - are you?", then you should get away with it; especially if they're deaf.

Mum and Dad are more of a problem. But there is a way out. And this is it: make sure that your room gets progressively less tidy as Christmas approaches. Resist all temptations to tidy it, however strong the urge becomes; however much your parents nag. Then, on Christmas Eve come rushing down the stairs[1] looking as distraught as you can possibly manage.

1: Unless you live in a bungalow.

At times like this it helps to think of something really really sad, like your little brother having a nasty accident with a combine harvester – no, sorry, that's a bad example – anyway, you'll think of something sad. Splash a bit of water on your face so that it looks like you've been crying, sweating, trying to drown yourself in the bath, etc. This will help. Having got yourself psyched to the correct level, burst into the lounge and say: "Mum! Dad! Have either of you been tidying my room, only I had some really expensive presents for both of you hidden in a secret place and THEY'VE GONE!"

At this point you may also want to say, "Oh," when you realize that your parents aren't in the lounge. You may then want to head for the kitchen, garden, bathroom, loo, etc, repeating the whole performance until you find them.

As long as you don't overdo it this should work perfectly. A word of warning though: make sure that you do this late at night so that there's absolutely no possibility of either parent saying, "That's OK – the shops are still open. You can nip out and get us something now." If you hear either of them say, "Sainsbury's is open ALL NIGHT!" throw yourself on the floor, being careful to hit the floor and not the dog, and sob uncontrollably. Even the most callous of parents will realize that you are far too upset to tackle anything as complex as shopping.

Lack-of-cash and lack-of-Christmas-present problems solved. But don't think you can relax; not buying people presents is going to be the *least* of your Christmas problems!

Let's open another Advent door...

Oh look! A robin on a log! Just before he gets eaten by the cat! Well, why shouldn't the cat have a treat? After all, it is Christmas, nearly. Apparently the reason that you get so many robins on cards at  Christmas is not because the garden is full of robins on Christmas day – although it might be.[1] The reason has to do with postmen. Apparently, postmen were originally called *Robins* because they wore red uniforms, and stood around on logs probably, and hopped about and whistled, and ate worms.

Maybe not! Anyway, robins eventually started appearing on Christmas cards. Isn't that interesting?

Agh!

That's another thing! Christmas cards – something else that can go horribly wrong. Even if you manage to buy enough cards you still run the very big risk of missing the last day for posting.

The last day for posting: one of the biggest mysteries of Christmas. Bigger even than the mystery of how the TV people think they can get away with showing *Chitty*

1: It might be but it's very unlikely.

Chitty Bang Bang every Boxing Day without anyone complaining. The great mystery about posting is that nobody seems to know how it works. The newspapers, radio and TV all seem to give out different information. Just when the *Sun* is telling you that you've missed your chance to send a parcel to the Falkland Islands, *Newsround* is assuring you that you can still get that power drill to your uncle on the planet Whaaargg. Who do you believe?

The short answer is nobody. The long answer is nobody as well. After all, the one big idiot-proof excuse for *not* sending cards is "I missed the last day for posting". Obviously this doesn't work if you're delivering the card by hand to a mate at school.

Oh yeah. School mates. One of the trickiest bits of Christmas card giving. Apart from the whole thing about "If I give them a card will they give me one? If I don't bother will they get upset?" etc., there's the much more important issue: cost. Christmas cards do not come cheap. Even the boxes that are marked "4,000 cards for 20p" are a false economy because they're so awful that your friends are going to hate getting them. The envelopes are thin enough for your mates to be able to see how awful the card is through them, and so often they don't even get opened!

I'm sure you know the kind of cards I'm talking about. They usually have a *nice* picture of a shop on them. A shop covered in snow. It's obvious that there's a secret message hidden in the picture; a subliminal reminder to get out there and spend all your money. Ironically these snowy shops are partially inspired by Charles Dickens' book *A Christmas Carol*. I say ironically because the book is all about a bloke who hates Christmas. Unfortunately he then has a series of very unpleasant nightmares, causing him to start throwing his money around with a careless abandon that would make even Richard Branson wince.

As clear a message from the big High Street stores as you're ever likely to get, I think you'll agree.[1] I only hope that the shops are all giving Dickens a decent cut of their profits.

But none of this is going to help you solve your card problem. You'll have made a list, just as you did with presents. You'll have then gone through the list crossing off relatives, brothers, sisters, neighbours etc., just as you did with the presents list. Unfortunately the list is still probably quite long, because one of the great things about sending a card is that it often means you don't have to send a present. You can even do the old "Did you get the fiver I put in your card? Oh dear! It must have fallen out" routine.

1: I.e. If you don't get thee out and spend, spend, spend you'll never have another decent night's sleep.

So, let's assume that you're staring at your Christmas list, which now largely consists of mates and school pals, but you still have no way of affording all those cards. There are several ways out of this situation. The main ones are:

1.

This works exactly as it sounds as though it might. The upside of this is that it can potentially save you a fortune. The downside is that your mates almost always see through it, mainly because they've thought of doing it themselves.

2.

Now this ploy is actually a good one. The only people who really lose out are the non-existent charity, who could probably do with a nice donation from you at Christmas. There are a couple of pitfalls to avoid though. Don't write to people explaining that you won't be sending them a card because you're going to donate the money to charity instead. This will probably cost you more than it would to send them a card in the first place! Also, avoid any conversation with your mates that starts to go along the lines of, "Brilliant idea! Why don't we all put our money together and send it all to charity *NOW*!" Again it might be cheaper to send them a card. And if you decide to do that, then why not send them a charity Christmas card? That way everyone gets the benefit.

3.

If you really are strapped for cash then this Blue Peter style ploy is the ideal solution. Unfortunately it involves a bit of forward planning, like keeping the cards from the previous Christmas, for instance. So if you've already thrown them away, then this is something to do *next* year. The way it works is like this: Let's assume that the card originally came from your Uncle Fred and Auntie Dot, and that they wrote, "Lots of love from Fred and Dot" inside. You take the card and write your name in between the word *from* and the word *Fred*. Then, underneath the original message you write *also send their love*.

The upside of this is that it will save you a fortune. The downside is that whoever you send the card to will spend the whole of Christmas wondering who Fred and Dot are, and worrying that they haven't sent them a card *back*. But then that's hardly your problem, is it?

Let's open another door. Gosh! Only 22 shopping days until Christmas!

Ah! A Christmas tree! Or Tannenbaum, as they'd probably say in Germany. After all, as I said earlier, the much loved and be-baubled Christmas tree was originally a German idea, brought to this country by Prince Albert, consort to Queen Victoria.

What did people think about the idea when he first suggested it, I wonder.

"In Germany ve chop down a tree and stick it in ze front room at Christmas."

"Do yer?"

"Oh ja – it is traditional."

The Victorians probably already thought Albert was a bit strange, what with him being German and everything.[1] This must have gone a long way to confirming it.

The big debate in most houses at Christmas is, "Shall we have a real tree or not?"

NOT – if you've got any sense.

Real trees cost a lot of money, their needles fall off

1: You must remember that the Victorians were doing their best to conquer the known world. Everything foreign would have been regarded with suspicion, even if it was married to the Queen.

after a couple of days, and then they sit in the back garden until somebody can be bothered to take them to the dump. You can try planting them, but then instead of looking like a dead Christmas tree lying in the garden, it looks like a dead Christmas tree *sticking out of* the garden.

The dustmen won't take them, in case they catch a very rare but fatal disease called Dead Christmas Tree Rot. This is a disease so deadly that even I can't describe it, even though I made it up!

Decorating the Christmas tree and the rest of the house is one of the great pre-Christmas rituals, isn't it? Your mum or dad climb into the attic and dig out the old suitcase containing the previous year's decorations.

Also in the case are all those decorations that you made when you were at play school; things that are so embarrassing now, but will your parents throw them away? – of course not! In fact, they insist on having these awful things on the tree, as a constant reminder of when you were *cute*.

Even when relatives and guests say things like, "Oh dear – your tree has been attacked by flying bits of rubbish!" your parents don't take the hint.

"Oh no! Geoffrey made that when he was three!"

"Really? Was he on heavy medication?"

It's bad enough having relatives pointing out that your having reached puberty was clearly against all odds, without having them dissecting your early attempts at handicraft.

You start to cringe; almost as much as you will when you open the gift they've bought for you and discover that it's socks.

Decorating the house is a family thing.

"Can I put up the streamers?" begs your little brother/sister.

"Oh no. That's far too dangerous," says Dad, trying to establish a great sense of mystery about this ancient ritual.

A voice inside you is screaming: "Please! Please let him/her climb that rickety old ladder that will barely take his/her weight! I don't mind spending Christmas visiting the hospital. It'd be worth it!" But you don't say anything. After all, Christmas is a time for being nice to little brothers and sisters. But don't worry, the amnesty need only last a few days.

So you lay out all of the tired old decorations. Having tried to make them look presentable by applying several rolls of sellotape, which ironically costs more than it would to completely replace the tattered streamers that have adorned your home since Cliff Richard was quite young.

The best job during this family operation is holding the ladder. It may not sound very exciting, but it's one of the few times that you get to make your dad look silly. How? I'll tell you... Set the ladder up just slightly too far away from where your dad intends to pin the end of the streamer. Dad won't notice this, and will lean over as far as possible without falling from the ladder (which is not something you need to let happen, by the way!). Having got himself precariously uncomfortable, he's bound to ask your advice.

"Is it straight?" he'll say, unable to make this judgement himself because he's too busy taking his life into his own hands.

"Hmm…" you say with the tone of an expert. "Let me see…"

"Hurry up!" cries Dad, gripping the ladder tighter than he would the safety bar on a white-knuckle ride.

"Erm … well, it could perhaps do with being a bit more to the … no, hang on … maybe…"

"Oh forget it! I'll do it myself!"

Hey presto! You've got out of putting up the streamers, which after all - let's face it - is a pretty mindless business, even if they do look nice when they're finished. Apparently.

Of course, a little extra thought can get you out of putting up the streamers *and* let you control what goes on the tree, thus allowing you to make sure that none of your childhood handiwork finds its way into the all-too-public glare of fairylight fame.

What you do is this...

As the battered suitcase of tattered Christmas trimmings arrives in the lounge, you say with as much "genuine" enthusiasm as you can fake: "Oooh! Let's do the streamers first! That's my favourite part!" (The *Oooh!* is optional, by the way.)

Then, having given your indecisive ladder-holding streamer-positioning expert performance, and your dad having dispensed with your services, you say: "I'll do the tree then, shall I?" and before anyone can stop you, you start decorating it. Your dad will be too busy trying to stay on the ladder to stop you, and the rest of the family will likewise be tied up preventing Dad from falling/ wobbling the ladder dangerously/checking his insurance policy etc. to bother about you.

You then have free rein to be as creative with the tree as you want to be, always making sure that you leave no branch uncluttered so that when your parents say: "Aren't you going to put that lovely Father

Christmas that you made at playschool out of a toilet roll tube and 37 Smarties on the tree?" you can say in all honesty: "Sorry, no room. Maybe next year." Maybe the year after. Maybe never!

Let's open the next little door.

Don't the darlings look angelic?

One very nice thing about Christmas is going to a real carol concert and hearing carols beautifully sung. There's no doubt about it, Christmas has got most of the best tunes. Unfortunately it doesn't always have all the best singers.

Imagine that you're settling down to watch your favourite TV show or play your favourite computer game, or you're just amusing yourself by confusing the dog.[1] Let's just assume that you're entertaining yourself in your favourite manner. Suddenly you hear the sound of somebody being murdered in a particularly messy and noisy way.

This time the victim is Good King Wenseslas, who never did anybody any harm as far as I can remember.

1: You can easily do this by putting your coat on and off; the dog will think you're going to take him for a walk, then he'll think you aren't, then you are, etc.; great fun. If you do it for long enough the excited jumping around should be enough exercise for your average mutt; and for you for that matter.

What's more, the crime is taking place on your doorstep.

You're alone in the house, apart from the dog.

"Quick," you say to it. "Burglars!"

The dog's tail starts going at a million miles an hour. He actually starts to propel himself around the room about six inches off the ground. He clearly thinks *burglars* is a new form of dog food.

But when the singers reach a particularly high bit, even the dog can no longer bear the noise.

So how do you get rid of them?

Paying them to stop is an option. But then, as we've already established, money is not a thing you have an awful lot of in the run-up to Christmas. As you're alone in the house you can't even threaten them with your parents, as in: "If you don't go away I'll get my mum to come and ruffle your hair."

Fortunately, there is a simpler solution.

You wait until you hear what sounds like a natural break in the carol, then throw open the door and say: "That was lovely. Can you sing me the next verse please?" You then stand on the step and wait. It helps if you can jingle some coins in your hand, just to

1: All he ever did was look out of the window and say "who's that?" as I recall – not a crime in any country as far as I know.

increase their enthusiasm and expectation. If you can't manage coins then something metal that sounds like money will do. But why would you want to do this? I'll explain...

It's a known fact that no door-to-door carol singers know the second verse. Oh yes, some enterprising (or desperate) choristers might make a brave stab at it, but they won't get any further than the first line.

At the point at which they start to shuffle their feet and look sheepish, you say: "Sorry – but I can't pay for half a carol", and close the front door, always making sure that you're on the *inside*. There's nothing more embarrassing than dismissing carol singers and then locking yourself out of the house. For one thing you'll probably find that one of them is just small enough to poke through an open window to get you back in again – at a price!

If the carol singers hang about once you're safely indoors with the door shut, make the dog bark (by your favourite method), and that should send them packing.

Time for another door.

 Hang on! *More* carol singers? That can't be right, surely. But it is. You'll discover as you go through Advent opening the little doors that your average poncy Advent calendar quickly runs out of suitable Christmas images. Or maybe they can't get hold of 25 different handcrafted chocolates. Whatever the reason, my research led me to discover that a lot of

Advent calendars are the same behind the little doors. I can only assume that the manufacturers did not consult each other about the contents of their calendars, which frankly is hardly in the spirit of Christmas, is it?

But since we've got ourselves a second helping of carol singers, let's consider carol singing. Doing it rather than listening to it this time.

This has always been a good way of making a few quid, which can come in handy in the cash-strapped days of pre-Christmas December.

But what about if you come up against somebody as crafty as you are? How do you get around that? Simple.

Imagine that you and your mates are singing as the punter opens the door.

"That was lovely," they say. "Can you sing me the second verse please?" (jingle, jingle).

"That *was* the second verse," you reply helpfully.

But they persist; they're not going to pay you if they can help it.

48

"Then sing the third verse."

"There *is* no third verse," you counter. "This particular version goes back to the first verse."

"Sing the fourth verse then."

"The fourth verse is an amalgam of verses one and two. Verse five is in Welsh and verses six, seven and eight are hummed. Of course, if you'd like to join in with verse nine, that's sung as a round."

You'll probably find that they pay up about halfway through this; if not you could offer to sing *Oh Christmas Tree* in the original German, with simultaneous translation, which goes something like "Oh fir tree, oh fir tree, how loyal are your leaves." It then goes on to say that no matter what the weather does the leaves never desert their tree. At which point the punter will probably give you all their credit cards as long as you promise not to come back. Ever.

Time for another little door.

It's Santa! I thought he would have turned up earlier than this. After all, some of the High Street shops have got him *in-store* from November. One store I went in had him so early that he was accompanied by the Easter Bunny.

But is it the *real* Santa?

Are any of them real?

Father Christmas as we know and love him was invented by the Americans. I think I mentioned this earlier. But what I didn't tell you was that he was originally dressed in green. So what turned him red?

Coca-Cola. By which I don't mean that he drank so much of the stuff that his clothes changed colour, although that might have happened. What I actually mean is that the Coca-Cola company changed his colour to fit in with their advertising campaign. Coke was originally packaged in green. When they decided to make it red, they re-launched it using Santa dressed in a red suit, and the red suit stuck. Talk about the power of advertising, eh?

But with so many Santas about, small children must get very confused. I know I do. One minute you're on his knee, wondering how such a spindly leg manages to hold up his massive weight – the next you're walking along the road and there he is again. Only now he's six stone, his beard's round the back of his head, he's puffing away at a cigarette and shaking a bucket in aid of cancer research. Well, I know that Santa is magic and can circumvent the globe leaving presents for all the children in the world (as long as they've been good) in one night, but that kind of weight loss is amazing. I always knew that smoking was bad for you.

I can only assume that there is more than one Santa and that none of these High Street Hairies are the real thing, although he might be in among them some-where, meeting and greeting his public. After all, if he didn't do a bit of that sort of thing, how would he keep in touch with the current trends in children's toys?

So assuming that the shop Santa is some retired actor wearing a false beard, what does the average visit to Santa's grotto actually entail?

For a start, let's look at the grotto itself. By and large these are extremely aptly named; *grot* meaning "rubbish" and *oh* being an exclamation of disappointed surprise. Of course, this isn't always the case. Some grottoes involve make-believe journeys to Lapland. Well, OK, you sit in a thing that looks like an open-topped train inside a "snowy" tent and listen to sound effects of a train journey. This alone should tell you that this is not a real train.

For a start there's no tea trolley with exotic but curly sandwiches full of weird combinations that you wouldn't even find mixed together in a bag of broken and spilled groceries: tuna, beetroot and kiwi fruit; egg and Marmite mayonnaise. There is also no vague public address system apologizing for the train being a day late – "this is due to us not giving a stuff". But as far as the wide-eyed infants who have yet to discover the great mysteries of real life are concerned, we are all going to Lapland to see Santa. When the sound effect finishes – sorry, when the journey ends (with a click as the tape is turned off) – we all pile off the "train" and form an orderly queue, grumpily supervised by an elf who looks remarkably like a girl who, less than a week ago, was working on the perfume counter.

It's reassuring to discover that, even in the magical world of Father Christmas Land, there's still queuing. One by one the excited children file into Santa's "inner sanctum". All right, they go behind a curtain, where Father Christmas himself is sat, resplendent in his Coca-Cola-red suit and elasticated face-fungus.

Having explained to the doting parent(s) that, due to an in-store memo, the children are not allowed to sit on his knee, "Santa" goes into the time-honoured ritual:

"Santa" clasps his perforated eardrum and mutters something not very festive. It's hard to tell exactly what it is through all that false beard material, but it certainly doesn't sound as though it has any more than four letters. Let's hope that this is *not* the real Father Christmas!

Recovering himself, "Santa" goes into his tick-list of questions:

A. HAVE YOU GOT A PET?
B. WHAT'S ITS NAME?
C. WHAT D'YOU WANT FOR CHRISTMAS?
D. HAVE YOU BEEN GOOD?

ER... COULD YOU REPEAT THE FIRST QUESTION?

The pet line of questioning is a desperate attempt at conversation. Santa has a pet, and therefore probably feels confident that he can chatter away with someone who is several generations younger with the ease that comes from having a common interest. Unfortunately Santa's pet is a red-nosed reindeer, and the chances of finding a kid with one of those, even in Harrods, are pretty slim. But at least the guy is trying.

We then come to the real reason why we're all here – "What do you want for Christmas?" This is said largely for the parents' benefit, the assumption being that the child hasn't already told their mum or dad a billion times that they want a *Thingy*.

The *Thingy* is this year's IN toy, according to the newspaper adverts paid for by the makers of the *Thingy*.

"It talks, it sings, it plays, it burps – in fact it's just like having a new baby brother!"

In fact, it sounds exactly like the sort of thing that no child in their right mind would *ever* want! But the papers say that everybody else wants one; and although nobody has actually met any of these "everybody else"s that the papers are referring to, *Thingy* is a MUST HAVE!!!

It's also an IMPOSSIBLE TO GET FOR LOVE NOR MONEY. Believe me, Mum and Dad have already tried. Well OK, maybe they haven't tried to get one for love, although Dad did threaten to kiss a shop assistant unless she sold him one. Not surprisingly, it didn't work.

Having established that the child wants whatever everybody else wants, Santa goes for the moral blackmail: "Yes – but have you been good?"

What possible answer is this man expecting?

"No. I've been appalling in every way that you can imagine and even a few that you can't."

I don't think so.

"Yes I have."

That's better.

Not that it will make any difference whatsoever, because Santa will then give the child something that is about as far removed from what it has asked for as it is possible to get. And if the management have got their act together it'll be something that requires batteries, a plug or a special string – all of which are available in the store at reasonable prices.

Of course, some poor kids will try and negotiate or remonstrate with "Santa", not realizing that a simple press on a neck-worn pendant will cause the child to be instantly surrounded by 85 armed security guards. And as he/she is carried screaming from the store and rammed into a *Help to Keep this Arndale Centre Tidy* bin, the first seeds of doubting the existence of Santa Claus will be sown.

Well, all I can say is – it's not HIM. Not the real HIM anyway. Santa would never be so horrible, even if you don't believe in him.

Of course, you are probably above such things. Your

days of sitting on Santa's knee and trying to pull his beard off, stopping only when he suddenly grips you in a "playful" Ninja Death-Lock, are long gone. But you may have a small brother or sister who is about to join the fantasy train – or at least the queue – to Santa Land.

This is your big chance to save them the humiliation and disappointment that a trip to Santa can so often bring. One word from you and you could prevent shattered illusions and parental wastage of money. Just one word. Or maybe one short sentence. Something along the lines of: "I wouldn't bother to go and see Santa if I was you." That's all you need to say. It's that simple, but it can save the breaking of a small brother or sister's heart.

The big question you should be asking yourself is: "Why would I want to do that, then?" You're right. Life's a learning curve. Let them find out for themselves. Unless, of course, you're paying!

 There must be those among you who have never made a snowman. When I say *snowman* I'm not talking about something that looks like two blobs of ice-cream held together with a stick, I mean a big six footer who looks like he's got a real obesity problem and a ludicrously high cholesterol level. Looking like that he should really go into hospital and have an operation. He could have a nose job at the same time – I'm not sure that trying to breath through a carrot is the best way to ensure a

long and healthy life. If you can call a life that only lasts until the sun comes out *long* that is. But for all that, he looks magnificent. He's something that Raymond Briggs would take one look at and say: "Wow! What a snowman! I must write a story about him!" At least, he would if he hadn't already done it. But why haven't some of you ever made a real snowman? It's not because you don't want to, although it might be; it's far more likely that you've just never had enough of the raw materials. By which I mean snow.

Where has all the snow gone? It used to be everywhere at Christmas. But now there are huge bits of the country that never get a single flake. There always seems to be plenty in Scotland. How many of us sit watching news footage of somebody in Fife digging a tunnel through the snow so that they can walk their dog, or somebody else pointing to an aerial sticking out of a drift and saying: "There's my car!"; and all we can think is: "Lucky devils!"

Every year the betting shops take bets on whether or not it'll be a white Christmas. The radio plays Bing Crosby singing: *I'm dreaming of a White Christmas*. Children everywhere ask their parents: "Who's Bing Crosby?" and their parents say: "Oh, he's just some dead bloke who sings *I'm Dreaming of a White*

Christmas every year." But none of this makes any difference, the snow still doesn't come. Maybe it's due to global warming, Government cutbacks or changing fashion. Who knows? All I can say is that I'm glad there's no snow.

One of the great myths of life is that snow is great. Oh yes, snow *looks* great. Snow on mountains to ski on, or on fields to play in is brilliant. But snow on the roads, pavements and anywhere that you need to walk is frankly a pain in the ... well, a pain in whatever you land on when you slip over in it. Because snow doesn't last. No sooner have you opened your mouth to say: "Oh goodie, Sn..." than you quickly have to change it to "Slush!", because that's what's happened to the snow. That crisp white blanket is now a muddy brown mush; the sort of thing that even your average School Dinner Lady couldn't describe as *appealing*. And believe me, they find most things attractive, particularly if it looks like they might just be able to force some poor unsuspecting child to eat it.

WEREN'T WE JUST WALKING THROUGH THIS IN THE PLAYGROUND?

But if snow didn't melt it would make things even more difficult. Let's face it, your average train service grinds to a halt if there's a leaf on the line, so how they'd cope with a six-foot snow drift is anybody's guess. So why is snow so popular? Because, as I mentioned earlier, it *looks* great. And centuries ago it was no problem. People went around in carts pulled by oxen who didn't need moon boots with heavy grips to get them through a drift; they knew a thing or two about walking in snow. And if they refused to budge the carter had a huge leather whip – ox leather probably – to encourage them. And so, as the ox plodded forward thinking "I'm sure I recognize that whip – it looks just like my brother Frank", the carter pulled his beaver skin hat down over his ears, safe in the knowledge that he'd reach his destination whatever the weather. But that sort of thing is just a distant memory. Today's snow is a different thing altogether. No – the best place for snow is on a Christmas card. And even then it can make you shiver.

Let's hope the next door has something a bit warmer behind it.

(AUTHOR'S NOTE: I wrote this bit of the book on Saturday 9 January, 1999. On Sunday 10 January, 1999 it snowed!)

Oh no! I think I prefer snow! What's a school doing in an Advent calendar? You'd think that would be one place where you could escape it, wouldn't you? But Christmas becomes a part of school life during December, and so I suppose that it's only fair to include it. The impact of Christmas on your education really depends on what sort of school you go to. In infant school the children are encouraged to make cards and decorations; the sort of thing that will come back to haunt them every year until they leave home. Teachers, in a desperate bid to prove that they too are capable of getting into the Christmas spirit (just about), cover the classroom windows with cotton wool balls intended to represent snow. The white ones *do*. It's the multi-coloured ones that cause the confusion. There must be hundreds of children going around thinking that snow is green, fluffy and falls on the *inside* of buildings. Because of the general snow shortage, they'll never know any differently. Ah well – that's education for you.

Apart from the decorations, these mixed-up infants are also encouraged to write to Santa. Fortunately Santa speaks several languages, including Gobbledee-Gook, and so he has no problem realizing that an *Akschun Monne* is that bloke with swivelling eyes and realistic gripping hands. Unless of course, the child wants a *Booby Dill*.

Secondary school is a different matter. After all, it would hardly be cool for a teacher to say, "Right, 9JC, for English today we're going to be writing to Santa." But they will erect as much in the way of decorations as the school budget will allow. So that'll be one plastic snowman and a bit of tinsel then.

Some schools take this opportunity to give their pupils a small gift; something that is practical and educational. I heard of one secondary school that gave each of its pupils a pencil, with the message

Nice idea! Merry Christmas! Unfortunately the pencil manufacturers had overlooked the fact that the pupils might want to *use* the pencil. And to do that they'd need to put a point on it. After a few sharpenings the message was:

A week or so later, just in time for Christmas, it was much more to the point:

Of course, you might think that Christmas is hard enough to cope with without it spilling over into your school life. And you'd be right. Unfortunately, you can't avoid it. Stay away from school and you'll be roped into the Christmas preparations at home. At least at school they aren't likely to make you peel the sprouts (but only because they haven't yet thought of it).

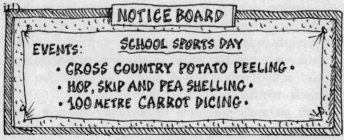

NOTICE BOARD

EVENTS: SCHOOL SPORTS DAY
• CROSS COUNTRY POTATO PEELING •
• HOP, SKIP AND PEA SHELLING •
• 100 METRE CARROT DICING •

Ah! The letter to Santa. If you don't do it at school you're going to be left to tackle this difficult task without the benefit of someone with a university degree breathing down your neck; unless your parents are educated. In which case, why do they behave so stupidly?

The letter to Santa is a tricky thing. How much do you ask for? After all, you don't want to appear too greedy, do you? On the other hand, if you leave anything off, does that mean that you're not likely to get it at all?

Having written it, how do you deliver it? The time-honoured method is to send it up the chimney.

I'VE POSTED MY LETTER

If you haven't got a chimney this obviously is a bit tricky. You can post it to him, of course, as long as you can pinch a stamp from somewhere.

Now you may be saying: "Why should I bother to write to Father Christmas?" The answer's simple – because it's traditional. It also ensures that your parents get the message about what you actually *want*. Believe me, parents are notoriously bad at taking the hint. Even if you tie them to a chair, make eye contact with them and say very slowly:

> READ MY LIPS – I WANT A BIKE FOR CHRISTMAS. HERE'S A PICTURE OF THE ONE I WANT AND IT'S IN THE WINDOW AT SAMSON'S CYCLES. IN FACT, MR SAMSON HAS PUT ONE BY FOR ME...

Even if you say all that, they'll probably still get it wrong. But if you show them your list, they'll be so keen to encourage you to believe that writing to Santa really works, that you're *bound* to get whatever you ask for. Maybe.

The accepted method of doing this is...

Write your letter to Santa, making a few simple spelling mistakes; the sort of thing that your mum or dad will spot without having to have them pointed out.

"Oh look – you've spelt *and* incorrectly."

"No. I think you'll find that I've spelt *that* incorrectly. I think you'll find that *and* really is spelt a-n-d."

The idea of the spelling mistakes is to ensure that your parent(s) study the letter really closely.

Another handy hint is to make the thing you really want more than anything slightly hard to read. This is so that your parent(s) will go:

"What's this? A smhasujyg?"

"No. That says personal stereo."

Be careful not to overdo the scrawliness in case it causes a parent's brain to explode.

Having got them to read it carefully, and maybe repeat it several times just to make absolutely sure they haven't missed anything, you should then say:

"Perhaps you'd like to post this for me, next time you go *shopping*."

If all this fails then maybe next year you should try asking Santa for a slightly better quality parent.

What on Earth is that lot? Oh – I know! It's *craftware*. The sort of stuff that some very talented and artistic people have spent the whole of the previous year knitting, sewing, whittling and welding so you can now *buy* it. Then give it to a relative for Christmas. Then watch their puzzled face as they try and work out what it is. For this is the very stuff of presents for relatives. And the place where you can buy it is called a Christmas Craft Fayre.

IT'S A JUMPER AND MAGNETIC CHESS BOARD

Schools sometimes organize these, in order to raise school funds. Your School PTFA[1] (if you're unfortunate enough to have one) may have one planned this year, or may be recovering from last year's. They will probably have held something similar in the summer, only without the cotton wool snow.[2]

Sometimes these are quite big events, requiring a lot of planning. The Head teacher will probably have sent a letter home to your parents asking for donations of tins, bottles and so on, which parents are then invited to bring into school. They are then invited to come into school at the weekend and buy their tins, bottles and so on back at the Christmas Fayre. You may think this sounds a bit of a rip-off, but frankly it serves them right for trying to get rid of their old rubbish and out-of-date tins of Spam in the first place.

Mr Wibley from the PTFA, who normally drives the Meals-on-Wheels van even though he's got a drink problem,[3] will be wearing his wife's old red flannelette dressing gown with hundreds of cotton wool balls superglued to his chin. A badly hand-written notice will tell you that this apparition is supposed to be

1: PTFA: Parents, Teachers and Friends Association. Most of them are parents; some of them are teachers; none of them are friends.
2: Although they may have had snow in the summer – they are very strange people!
3: Maybe *problem* is too strong a word. He drinks, he falls over. Not really a problem.

Father Christmas. He is in his "Grotto" – AKA the cleaners' broom cupboard. As with last year, someone has forgotten to take the brooms out, and so several unsuspecting visitors to Santa's grotto find themselves leaving with a coloured pencil set and a huge bruise on the back of their head, products of a cheapskate Santa and a falling mop handle.

And of course, there's a raffle. First prize a gift certificate, exchangeable at the local hospital for a hip operation. You will have been sent home with several books of raffle tickets, with strict instructions to make sure you sell them unless you want to spend the rest of your life doing quadruple homework; those nice PTFA people can be very persuasive.

So what – you find yourself asking – am I doing here? Simple. You're in the school choir. Someone, the music teacher to be exact, has volunteered you to sing carols. How could she refuse? The PTFA had her dangling upside down over the piranha-infested school terrarium. How did they get in there? It started life as an ant farm! They were probably another thoughtful gift from the PTFA. It's amazing what all that fund-raising can do! Anyway you've been practising all week – *We Three Kings* with all the right words; no mention of a scooter or a car. Teacher has promised that if you do well you'll all get to go and sing to the old people in the Bideawee Home for Incontinent Gentlefolk. As if being in a home wasn't bad enough, without having a load of kids screaming at you. Anyway, it's possible that you won't get to sing at the Christmas Fayre even. After all, the infant recorder choir are performing first – *Lord of the Dance* for anyone who doesn't recognize it. Any parent who survives that will almost certainly be able to take *We Three Kings* sung in a key that, until this moment, didn't actually exist.

Why do teachers make you do this? Isn't Christmas meant to be the season of good will? How much – or rather how *little* – good will will be left by the time you get to the bit about "star of wonder, la la la".[1]

Don't worry – help is at hand. That nice Mrs Juicefoot has brought the hall to deadly and stoney silence by screaming "It *is* a fund-raising event, you know!" Apparently some scrooge-like grandmother has pointed out that £7 for a cup of tea and two chocolate digestives is a bit steep. Aware that all eyes are on her and the argument is being lost, Mrs

1: Not the actual words I realize, but probably the ones you'll all end up singing.

Juicefoot quickly recalls her childhood black-belt Karate training. One broken window, an arm and two legs later the Craft Fayre is continuing as before, apart from the additional and distant wail of an ambulance. So reassuring to know that they are still working this close to Christmas. Meanwhile, the gentle raffia egg-cosy makers, the plywood-teddy-badge carvers and the dried-flower pressers are doing a roaring trade, as very small children press hard-earned pennies into the silky hands of craftspersons.

The fundraiser has been a huge success; it has raised over £1000. The school will get much-needed equipment, and anyone who bought anything from the hotdog stall will get salmonella.

A job well done, you are just refreshing your vocal chords with a can of Father Christmas-red Coke, when you hear the bad news. Your singing date at the Bideawee Home has been cancelled, due to a sudden high rate of fatalities among the "inmates". Apparently, because the home is only across the road, they could hear the school choir singing at the Craft Fayre, and started throwing themselves out of the windows.

And talking of windows, let's open another one…

Christmas is a time for pets too, unless your pet is a turkey. But many people make the mistake of getting a pet for someone at Christmas. This is usually a result of not really knowing what to buy them.

"I couldn't see anything I thought you'd like, so I got you a tarantula."

Nice.

You may even be tempted to ask Santa for a pet for Christmas; a dog, for instance. Yes, I know it's a nice thought. A little fluffy bundle of your very own to love and care for. But before you write "Dear Santa, can I have a bog"– that's meant to be dog, but I was assuming that you would misspell it for your parents' benefit – "please?" think about it. Once you get the Christmas wrapping off, that little dog will need feeding, cleaning, training, walking, loving, chiding and a whole lot of other things that will take up most of your precious free time. One way to avoid this is not to take the paper off in the first place, but that might turn out to be more distressing than having a dog ruining your life.[1]

Sorry, but dogs don't make good Christmas presents. They won't sit still under the tree for a start.

1: Particularly when it starts to smell.

70

12 December. 13 days to go. Ignoring superstition, it's about this time that teachers start to think about the true meaning of Christmas: two weeks without having to teach other people's kids. No, sorry, I meant the Christmas message; the story of Jesus. In primary schools, subtly at first, the story of Jesus will be introduced into lessons:

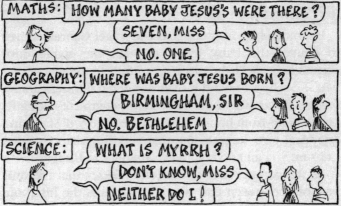

MATHS: HOW MANY BABY JESUS'S WERE THERE?
SEVEN, MISS
NO. ONE

GEOGRAPHY: WHERE WAS BABY JESUS BORN?
BIRMINGHAM, SIR
NO. BETHLEHEM

SCIENCE: WHAT IS MYRRH?
DON'T KNOW, MISS
NEITHER DO I!

All this religious education will be brought to a head, probably literally, with the school play. *Minutes* of careful planning will have gone into what is going to prove to be the dramatic highlight of the year. Shepherds will be wearing their own dressing gowns, turned inside out to cover up Thomas the Tank Engine. No one will be able to dry any dishes all week, because every tea towel in the neighbourhood will be tied to a small child's head with a snake belt. Did they really go around with tea towels on their heads in Jesus' time?

71

And so to the actual event. Doting parents will be crammed into the school hall. After a pleasant request from the headteacher not to take photographs during the performance, parents will start taking photographs during the performance.

Hearts will be in mouths as the Angel Gabriel arrives to deliver the baby Jesus, through the stable door surprisingly.[1] Will she place it carefully in the manger, or will she refuse to hand it over like she did in rehearsals?

After the arrival of the three kings, complete with gifts on cushions from home, the Head Teacher will stand and say: "And now let's all sing that very popular carol that I'm sure you all know so well, *Away in a Manger*."

As the parents start to sing she realizes that the only part of her speech that was accurate was the bit about the carol being very popular, although it won't be for long if it has to rely on parents like these to keep its memory alive!

I hope none of this is bringing back memories to make you shudder with embarrassment. Many of you will have been that Gabriel, or one of those tea-towelled shepherds, or the Wise Man who was foolish enough to drop his gift.

1: This is a very unusual method of delivering a baby, as I'm sure you realize. I'm not even sure it's historically accurate.

And one day you might be one of those parents. You'll be sitting proudly watching your son or daughter perform. You'll be ignoring requests about photos and fluffing the carol singing.

Of course, you could avoid the whole thing by giving your child the day off school. But surely you wouldn't want them to miss it? It'd be one less memory for them to squirm about. But you'd be better advised to learn the words of *Away in a Manger* before you reach parenthood. They're bound to sing it. Just after the recorders finish.

The big question is: were they kings or wise men? Or  both? Or neither? You don't have to be wise to be a king. And just because you're a king it doesn't make you more clever. Take our very own lovely Queen. She's quite clever I expect, but I bet she doesn't know how to rollerblade; or the best way to harden conkers. But then she's not like you and me, is she? She's thinner than I am for a start. And shorter. I think. I don't really know. In fact I don't really know much about her, any more than the people in Jesus' time knew much about the Three Wise Men. Or Kings. If they *were* kings which countries were they kings of? They came from the East, but whereabouts exactly? Perhaps they weren't real kings after all. Perhaps they were wise men. But how wise is it to start following a star? If you follow a star in Hollywood you can get arrested for stalking. Oh no - that's the wrong kind of star, isn't it? Nevertheless I can't see the wisdom in

73

following a star. After all, if they were that wise they'd know that stars don't move about. Not normally anyway. So this was no ordinary star. But maybe they were no ordinary wise men. Or kings.

One thing is certain though: whoever they were, the effects of their visit to Jesus are felt very strongly today. Just think about the gifts they bought him for a start: Gold – a precious metal, Frankenscence – a perfume, and Myrhh – an ointment. Just the sort of gifts you get today, except that now it's cash, scent and spot cream. Those three kings – or wise men – have got a lot to answer for.

And talking of parties, Christmas is a time when we get more than our fair share, isn't it? More than we really want probably. It all starts with the school party. The school very generously throws a  huge party for us. This is usually shortly after the school cook has given us a special Christmas dinner with all the trimmings; I think it's the school's way of saying sorry. But actually they don't really *give* the party, do they? What they usually do is write to our mums and dads saying that they are giving us a party (very generous) and would they send some party food in (very cheeky). So what do our parents do? They go through the cupboards picking out all the stuff they want to get rid of, stick it in a carrier bag and we hump it into school.

"Hang on!" you should say. "I can't eat this stuff!"

"Don't worry. Somebody else will eat it."

I don't know about you but I don't know *anybody*

who can stomach tinned ravioli. It's like packets of noodles without the taste.

But all this stuff gets piled on to a table, and somebody – somebody with magic powers probably – turns it into a Christmas "feast". And we eat it! How? Maybe by then we're so stewed up about Christmas that we'd eat anything. Let's face it, you need to get a bit of practice at eating weird stuff because Christmas is full of it.

When you're at primary school the party often boasts a Children's Entertainer, somebody who'd never get a job in the real world. This is usually a magician and I think the idea behind employing him is that you'll be so busy trying to work out which sleeve he's got the rabbit up that you won't think about the hideous food trying to get itself digested in your stomach.

I think these children's magicians are in league with tinned ravioli people. They employ them to make sure that the ravioli gets eaten.

Sorry – I'll have to stop for a minute. The milkman has just delivered the Christmas hamper.

I'm back, and I've checked. There's plenty of tinned ravioli in it. Goody. That can go to the local school next Christmas. Tinned chicken – that's another one. That stuff has never been anywhere near a chicken. I doubt that it's even been shown a *picture* of one.

If you hear your parents saying: "Shall we get a hamper this year?" try to put them off, otherwise you'll be spending the whole of February and March trying to digest sandwiches made from stuff in tins that is definitely not of this world.

Anyway – the party. The magician is nearing his climax as 50 per cent of his young audience are sick. The magician looks relieved. After all, this is a bigger finish than anything *he* could pull out of a hat.

Christmas, as we've already established, is a time for many things: giving, receiving, singing, praying, not to mention good will. Not to mention also eating strange stuff. I say not to mention it, but that's precisely what I'm going to do. In fact, I'm going to talk about it at some length.

There are certain things that you wouldn't really dream of eating at any time other than Christmas. Pickled walnuts for instance. Actually I wouldn't dream of eating them at any time, *even* Christmas. But that's the weird thing. Stuff you wouldn't look twice at any other time of the year you scoff down because it's there.

Some of it is traditional: Christmas Pudding dates back to pre-Christian times when it was a sort of muddy soup with all sorts of meat in it. Any unsuspecting animal who happened to wander past the window when it was being made found himself a part of the whole experience.

But what about stuff like bread sauce? Cranberry sauce? What's all that about? Crikey – by the time you get everything on your plate that is supposed to be a part of the traditional Christmas dinner you've hardly got the strength to eat any of it. That's presumably why Christmas dinners used to last about nine hours. But what's it all about? The trouble is that relatives go into a sort of feeding frenzy, don't they? Not content with scoffing anything on their plate they start looking around for other delicacies:

"Shall we have a cracker?"

"I'm not sure I could manage another thing. Oh all right – just the one."

You do your best to point out that it's made of cardboard, but too late! It's gone and you didn't even get to look at the joke.[1] And now they've started on the tablecloth!

There's really nothing you can do about this. Just try and make sure that you don't get sucked into it... Just a minute. I'd never noticed how plump and succulent the cat looked before. Excuse me...

1: So some good came out of it, then.

Ah, that's another really strange thing about Christmas. What's with all the berries? You know, holly, ivy, mistletoe – all that stuff. (OK, so ivy doesn't have berries, but why let that stand in the way of a good argument?) Take mistletoe for a start: we hang it up and snog under it. But why is that? There are various explanations, but the one I like best concerns the Norse Goddess of Love and Marriage, Frigga. Not that you have to love somebody in order to snog them, any more than you have to marry them, but there is a romantic connection. Now according to legend Frigga's son Baldur was killed but came back to life. When he did so, Frigga cried tears that turned into the berries on mistletoe. Unfortunately he was later killed again, ironically by a blind man waving a sprig of mistletoe! True. Well, myth anyway.

The ancient Druids worshipped mistletoe and the Victorians believed that it symbolized surmounting all obstacles, but it's probably because of Frigga and Baldur that we kiss under it. Of course, it wasn't made of plastic in those days.

Holly was the ancient Roman symbol of friendship and was often given as a gift.

But according to folklore (whoever they are) you should never bring holly into the house before Christmas Eve because it causes family quarrels. So that's what's doing it, then?

Holly also repels lightning apparently.

But what about ivy? Nice girl, terrible teeth. But the plant was worshipped by the ancient Egyptians for its medical properties. It was supposed to cure most things. The Greeks were also pretty keen on it and used to make crowns out of it for their conquering heroes.

So if anyone wonders why you're putting holly and ivy all over the house, just tell them "it's traditional".

Actually, you could use that argument for almost anything.

One of the other great fixtures of the school Christmas calendar is the School Disco. Brilliant! A real chance to let your hair down, not to mention the fact that there's this girl (or boy) in Year Nine who's absolutely...

"Well, I'll see you all at the disco tonight. Class dismissed."

WHAT?!? Surely teachers aren't allowed at school discos? It must be in the school rules, surely.

Apparently it isn't and apparently they are.

Well, that's going to put a whole new slant on things, isn't it?

Looks like you're not going to need that mistletoe after all. Why do teachers do that? They give you a real treat by organizing a disco and then go and spoil it all by turning up themselves. Of course, they're not all there to spy on you and make sure you behave yourself. Some of them are there to have a good time. And they are the worst! They turn up in what they imagine is the latest gear; well, it *was* the latest gear when they bought it. Unfortunately they bought it in 1983.

They haven't got the hang of the latest dances, which is amazing because they're not that tricky.

There's no way *you're* going to get to dance tonight. Not if it means sharing the floor with *them*! And dancing is mainly what you want to do; mainly. Well, let's face it, you're not going to get a chance to do anything else are you? Not with half the staff stood round the walls checking for anything other than normal contact.

THERE WAS SOMETHING IN HER EYE, MISS!

YES, SIMPKINS YOUR FACE!

Strangely enough this is where the mistletoe might come in handy because it gives you the perfect excuse for a snog. If any teacher tries to stop you, you just say: "But it's traditional. We've *got* to do it." You could even try adding: "We wouldn't go within five miles of each other normally."

Of course that might be stretching credibility just too far. After all, these are teachers. They may be from another planet but they're not stupid. The only thing you have to watch with this line of argument is that the teacher doesn't say: "Oh well, if it's traditional…" and try to join in!

Hello – what's this? Not another school is it? I couldn't bear it! Oh no – it's a house. It's quite likely that after the school disco you'll break up for Christmas. Teachers like to arrange things that way so that you pupils have a couple of weeks to forget all about how embarrassing they looked on the dance floor.

The Christmas holidays! Brilliant! After the long winter term, with mock exams and all sorts of other horrible stuff, you're just about ready to collapse into a big armchair, put your feet up and wait for Christmas to wash over you like a huge, warm tidal wave that smells of sage and onion. What a wonderful thought!

Think again.

You've got relatives coming for Christmas and with typical parental logic your mum points out that the entire house has got to be cleaned from top to bottom; and side to side; and inside and out. Every tiny minute corner has got to be spotless. Why?

"Because your Auntie Doreen is coming."

Now it has to be said that your Auntie Doreen's house is spotless. It's like one of the show homes that you get on new housing estates. You know the sort of thing: fully furnished down to a loo roll in the bathroom but nobody actually lives in it.

"But that's the way Auntie Doreen likes to live," you point out with more than a bit of common sense, if you don't mind me saying. "Even Auntie Doreen must realize that most other people like to live *normally*."

But your words, I'm afraid, have fallen on deaf ears. Your mother is even now loading a mop with industrial strength floor cleaner which she will then wipe over the entire house, including floors, walls, furniture and the dog. In the case of the dog it might improve the smell, although I doubt it.

This kind of excess would be fine if it wasn't for the fact that your mum expects you to join in, with the same adrenalin-driven fervour that she is demonstrating.

Why, just because Auntie Doreen is staying, do you have to clean the *inside* of your own bedroom cupboard? What do your parents expect Auntie Doreen to do – pull out a Swiss army knife, and remove all of the fitted cupboards to inspect for traces of dust? And more especially, why *your* bedroom cupboard?

"Because your Auntie Doreen is having your room."

"Oh, right."

Pause, during which you take in what has just been said.

"WHAT???!!!???"

"You heard."

Yes, you did hear. You heard perfectly. Hearing isn't the problem. Coming to terms with what has just been said is the problem. Auntie Doreen is having your room for the entire Christmas period. Not only will you not be in your own cosy bed surrounded by your own cosy things, you'll also have nowhere to escape to when Christmas becomes impossible to take, which it will; it *has* to – it's traditional.

Although of course you might have somewhere to go; they haven't told you where you're sleeping yet.

"So where am I sleeping, then?"

This provokes a long and complicated explanation of the masterplan of the sleeping arrangements.

From which you learn a number of things. The key bits of which are:

a) More relatives than can logically be fitted into a three-bedroomed house have been invited.

b) But don't worry, your parents have spent hours shuffling and reshuffling bedrooms until everyone has been accommodated. Everyone has somewhere to sleep.

c) Except you.

"Where am I going to sleep?" you say, sounding slightly aggrieved, which frankly I don't blame you for one little bit. I think you deserve to be aggrieved. I would be if it happened to me (again).

"Don't worry. We'll think of somewhere."

Why is it that parents always manage to make you feel as though you're being difficult, when all you want to know is whether or not you're going to have a bed for the next couple of weeks. They manage to do the same thing if you say a simple thing like "What's for tea?"

"Don't worry," they say, "you're not going to starve," and then promptly forget about you for a couple of days. But food is not going to be the problem over Christmas. Having somewhere to lie down when your stomach feels like it's going to burst might be. Although you should take some comfort from the fact that your parents have said "Don't worry – we'll *find* somewhere."

The downstairs loo would not be my first choice as a temporary bedroom, I have to say. Apart from the fact that it's where the cats' litter tray is kept, and cats are notorious for spending half of the night relieving themselves, there's also the fact that every member of your family over 30 suffers from weak bladder syndrome. If you were to put a turnstile on the loo door you'd be able to retire to the Bahamas by the time you were 20.

But your parents don't seem to realize this as they press the sleeping bag you had when you were in the cubs/brownies (or was it the beavers?) into your hand and say: "You'll be very comfortable and there's a radiator in there." Yes – it's the one that makes a clanking noise all night.

"Lucky you," says Dad with a logic that not even someone who'd won a Nobel Prize for Logic could begin to work out. "I'd sleep in there myself if it wasn't for the fact that I can't see the point of paying the mortgage and then sleeping on the lavatory floor."

Oh nice one, Dad! That's a neat variation on the old *I pay the bills so I call the shots* argument.

So this is going to be Christmas: sleeping on the toilet floor and getting trampled by assorted distant relatives every half hour; plus watching them, and the cats, performing something that should be a very private function. Who says there's no Santa Claus?

 It doesn't matter how many photos you look at of relatives, when you see them in the flesh (and there's usually plenty of it) you still want to say "Who are you?" Or even "WHAT are you?"

Just before the relatives arrive Mum and Dad will get out the family album, carefully flicking past pictures of themselves in flares with afro hair, then pointing other people out: "Look that's your Auntie Doreen paddling on the beach at Frinton." When you meet her you just can't imagine her paddling. She looks more like the sort of person who would have to be asked to leave the beach because the tide was frightened to come in.

The cruellest thing of all is cousins; particularly cousins about your age of the opposite sex. These were the ones you tortured as a child, safe in the knowledge that they would grow up ugly and be sent to live on another planet. Unfortunately they always grow up extremely *fit* and they always come back to haunt you. You are doomed to spend Christmas wondering whether they remember how close to death you brought them on numerous occasions, and whether they mind. And whether they fancy you. And if they do fancy you whether you will ever be able to be alone with them. Your personal private space is now the downstairs loo, remember!

Unfortunately they have something else they didn't have when you last knew them. In addition to their stunning looks, they now have a younger brother/ sister whose express purpose in life is to make yours (and everybody else's) a total misery. Yes – it's going to be a typical family Christmas. You're going to really enjoy yourself.

The older relatives are true to form. Why is it that aunts and uncles who haven't seen you for years are *amazed* that your appearance has changed.

"My, how you've grown!"

How did they expect you to grow? *What* did they expect you to grow – another head? They certainly seem to have done just that, only they've cunningly hidden it up the front of their hand-knitted jumper.

"I can't believe that you're 13. You used to be five."

That's another stupid thing they say. And for the whole of Christmas they'll question everything you do.

"Could you pass the carrots, please?"

"You're not having more carrots are you!?!"

And if you don't ask them to pass the carrots they'll say:

"Not having any carrots? You'll never grow up like me!"

You think, but obviously you can't say, that your dearest wish is *not* to grow up like them.

Thank heavens for Uncle Frank! He's always been the life and soul of the party. The pranks you and he got up to when you were younger – *Frank's Pranks* he used to call them. If anyone is going to salvage this family Christmas it's going to be him. You can almost bear having to sleep in the downstairs loo, safe in the knowledge that Frank will make the grey skies blue.

"You don't remember me, do you?" says the grumpiest man you've ever seen in your life.

You want to say "I don't think so? You're not that serial axe murderer that *Crimewatch* have asked us all to look out for are you?" but naturally you don't. You just shuffle your feet slightly and try to look interested.

"I'm your Uncle Frank. And I might have something for you. But only if you've been good."

Ah. It starts to dawn on you. This is one of *Frank's Pranks*. He's wearing an extremely well-fitted latex grumpy old man mask, and when you reach out your hand to take whatever it is he's got for you, his hand will come off and reveal itself to be one of those rubber ones with fake blood all over the stump. Or maybe it'll actually come off for real – Uncle Frank's like that; he'll go to any lengths for a gag, even amputation.

But no. Frank presses a coin in your hand, which you instantly recognize as a ten pence piece; a real one; no hidden explosive devices or elastic attached to make it disappear as you try to pocket it.

This is definitely a joke. But where's the punchline?

"Aren't you going to say thank you, you ungrateful child?"

Oh. This *isn't* the Uncle Frank you remember. Perhaps he never had a sense of humour, or maybe he left it on a bus on his journey through life.

Either way you are not going to be able to rely on him to be your Christmas saviour.

That evening you try to arrange all the various items on the floor of the downstairs loo so that the sleeping bag will be vaguely flat. It's a puzzle that Doctor Rubik would be proud to have invented; it could even be next year's Christmas blockbuster toy.

One of the cats comes in. Oh well, at least you'll have a bit of company for the night you think as the cat...

Oh dear! I thought the dog was supposed to be the smelly one!

That's something you don't see an awful lot of at Christmas – a friendly shop; one that doesn't look like it's just staying open so that it can relieve you of your money (and possibly your parents' money too).  You also don't see many covered in snow, because

a) snow is rare;

b) lots of shops these days have such sophisticated central heating that the minute anything like snow or rain hits the shop front it boils up hot enough to make coffee. (They also have these blow heaters fitted above the door, so that if you pause for a split second as you leave the shop you get a light tan.)

The shops that aren't like this are so cold, and you have to move around so much just to keep warm, that you run the risk of getting arrested for behaving suspiciously. Bearing this in mind the last thing you want to hear is one of your parents saying: "I think we need a few things from the shops."

OK so the relatives have eaten more than anyone could have possibly predicted, even if they were as gifted in the predicting department as Mystic Meg. Uncle Frank even took a bite out of the dog, but only because he walks and eats in his sleep.

I don't know what your definition of *a few things from the shops* is, but mine would probably include something like a loaf and some milk. Your mum now produces a list so big that you'll be lucky to get it in a whole *convoy* of supermarket trolleys.

"Would you like me to go with you?" asks Gorgeous

Cousin. Your preferred answer is: "I'd like you to shop instead," but since this could be a *being alone* opportunity, you readily agree.

Unfortunately, when you get to the supermarket, you realize that you are anything but alone – the place is totally packed.

What are all these people doing here? And why are they buying so much stuff? Don't they know that the shops will all be open on Boxing Day? 24 hours – that's all the time they'll be shut. You couldn't get through the amount of stuff most of these people are buying in a *month* let alone 24 hours! Why do they need it? What do they think is going to happen? Is Parliament suddenly going to be recalled from their holidays in the Seychelles to pass a law, effective immediately, to prevent anyone leaving their house on pain of death? Of course not! Most politicians don't even make their kids go back to school on the first day of term. So they're hardly likely to pass such a nasty law. I can only assume that people are buying loads of stuff because *they've seen other people doing it*. They've been in a shop, seen somebody panic-buying, and instead of saying: "That's a silly idea" they've said: "I'd better do that!"

None of this would matter if it wasn't for the fact that you have been dragged into this whole stupid situation. And as you try to have a half-decent conversation with Gorgeous Cousin, re-living childhood memories, carefully avoiding all references to near-death experiences, you are being pipped to the last punnett of pineapples, chased from the cheese counter and jostled by the joints of beef. It's going to take *hours* to get all the stuff on this list. *Days* even. Christmas could be a distant memory by the time you get home. Even when you get to the checkout queue the end is not in sight.

The various supermarkets *know* that the checkouts are very slow at Christmas. To counteract the negative effect of this they pass out mince pies. Service is so slow in this particular supermarket that they're passing out camp beds; some of the shoppers are just passing out.

...yells a normally friendly pensioner, jabbing you in the back.

"What happened to the spirit of Christmas?"

"Christmas? Humbug!"

Oh no! That's something on the list that you've forgotten to get!

Many people try to avoid the stress of a family Christmas by going to visit somebody else for the holidays. Unfortunately the people you visit are usually relatives, so although you might get out of some of the stress of preparing for the event, you still cop for the stress that goes with being surrounded by your family. It's also a known fact that if you visit a relative at Christmas, your parents will pick one who nobody likes and who lives somewhere that is almost impossible to reach without a team of huskies and a light aircraft. Why do they do that? Why does nobody ever say to the next door neighbour: "Why don't you come to us this Christmas and we'll come to you next year." Mainly, I suppose, because nobody speaks to their neighbour from one year's end to the next, and there's nothing to suggest that Christmas is going to be any different. Perhaps that's what people mean when they say, "We had a very *quiet* Christmas"; they mean that they weren't talking to each other.

I'M NOT MAKING THE FIRST MOVE, IT'S NOT MY FAULT!

Anyway, despite protests from you, your parents are determined to go to second cousin Vera's for the Christmas break. Because of the huge amounts of clothes, presents, food etc that they insist on taking with them, the plan is to throw everything in the back of the car and just go.

RIGHT, IS THAT EVERYTHING?

YOU FORGOT THE FOUR WALLS AND THE ROOF!

Unfortunately the Government have chosen this week to launch their drink-driving campaign, and so your parents announce:

"We're going by train."

Don't they realize that you've got far less chance of having a car accident than you have of boarding a train to Scotland and winding up in Devon? Besides, this time of year the railways are fraught with hazards that make drunken drivers seem almost attractive; leaves on the line for instance.

"We're sorry for the late departure of this train. This is due to unforeseen weather conditions."

What are they on about, bad weather? It's blazing sunshine, a heat wave in the middle of December. The announcement continues and explains.

"This is due to the driver feeling a bit hot in the cab.

He has just nipped home to take his vest off."

Oh well, we can all sympathize with that, can't we? There's nothing worse than feeling a bit hot, even if you do put 1,200 passengers' Christmases at risk. Mind you, it'll take more than one train driver to ruin Christmas. But don't worry – there *will* be more; much, much more!

But at least you're staying at home this Christmas, so you'll be able to fight it on home ground. You won't win, but at least you'll be on home ground.

Well, everything's as ready as it's ever going to be; i.e. not at all. With Christmas just a few days away it's time to take a stroll round town, look at the lights, dodge the charity Santas. They are everywhere. Not that you'd mind giving to charity, if you hadn't already pumped what little money you had into gifts for unappreciative relatives. You know exactly what'll happen: they'll unwrap it, say "that's nice dear," and promptly forget to take it home with them. Mind you the upside is that you can always give it to them again next year. They won't realize.

I'M GOING FOR A RECORD "SIXTH YEAR" WITH THIS PRESENT TO MY AUNTY MAY

As the various Santas jingle their charity tins, small children say things like: "Why is Santa begging, mummy? Hasn't he got any money?" Christmas must be very confusing for little children. Aren't you lucky you're old enough to understand it all? If you do, perhaps you could explain it to me.

You've been given strict instructions to keep the relatives out of the house while mum has her pre-Christmas breakdown. Why is she allowed to have one, while you have to hold it all together? That can't be fair, surely?

Anyway, you've been snaking through the town like an outing from an old folks home. You can tell that people feel sorry for you because when Uncle Frank's hat blew off passers-by started dropping coins into it. You make a mental note of this as a way of raising cash next year. Unfortunately, it'll mean getting mum to invite Frank a week early, but it might be worth it.[1] Suddenly you have a brainwave. Of course!

"Would you like to go and see the charity lights in Pargetta Grove," you suggest.

"How much is it?" asks Aunty Doreen, who has always been so careful with her money that you'd think that she'd be able to afford to look slightly less like a bag-lady.

"As much as you like. It's for charity."

1: It won't, believe me. Resist the temptation!

Your family all take their arms out of their sleeves and thrust them down inside their coats so that it looks as though they haven't got any in that endearing way they have of avoiding spending money, and agree to join you.

The Pargetta Grove Lights have become a local attraction. So popular that they now have their own AA sign and everything. They started a few years ago when Donald Campion, a local businessman and resident of Pargetta Grove decorated the outside of his house with Christmas fairy lights. He'd been on a business trip to the States and had been impressed by the way they do it "on the other side of the pond", as he was fond of saying. Unfortunately, that first year he rather overdid it and every home in a 200 hundred mile radius was plunged into darkness. But everyone agreed that it looked very nice. It was almost worth being forced to cook and eat Christmas dinner by candlelight that Christmas. There were a few complaints, but Donald got around those by placing a kiddies' potty on the front lawn with a sign saying *For Charity* on it.

"What kind of charity is gonna want a kid's potty?" asked a few grumpy souls who hadn't quite got into the spirit of it.

After taking out the cost of electricity, equipment, "sundry expenses" etc, Donald was able to donate the princely sum of £23.74 to a local retirement home – Dunworkin' (prop: Mrs Maureen Campion [no relation, only his sister]). But more importantly, the notion of a street full of Christmas lights for charity was born.

The following year Donald was able to persuade more of the residents of Pargetta Grove to decorate their homes. He was also able to sell them the equipment, having only that week branched out into the Christmas novelty lighting business. Soon most of the grove was festooned with light-up Wise Men, flashing shepherds and singing Virgin Marys. In fact, only one house has so far resisted the temptation to join in; the bungalow at the end, where the Reverend and Mrs Jenkins live.

"I don't know what's wrong with the man," complains Donald to anyone who'll listen. "He doesn't seem to know the meaning of Christmas."

Donald, on the other hand, has really expanded operations. He has converted his loft into an observation platform, and for as little as £20 you can sip mulled wine and watch the story of the nativity revolve in front of you. He'll even point out the very spot where his dog Herod ate next door's cat.

His sister has been able to open another three retirement homes and a holiday cottage on the island of Mustique, where the only old person she bumps into is Mick Jagger.

You can even get a hot dog, now that the street traders have moved in. Donald feels that this has spoilt the atmosphere.

"Frankly we could well do without them – and the charity Santas."

Only two days to go before THE BIG DAY, and the women are gathering in the kitchen. There are four generations of them; five, if you count the cat. But what are they doing? They're debating the most important issue at Christmas time – when to start defrosting the turkey. Why only women? Surely in this age of equality men should be allowed a say too? After all, the men are going to eat it as well. But no, when the men were invited to have their say, they refused on the grounds that defrosting the turkey is a women-only tradition. And Christmas is steeped in tradition, which I'm sure you've realized by now.

In the days before "frozen" was the normal way to buy food (and "fast" was the way to eat it), you got your turkey at the last minute from the butcher. You then removed its head and feet; this was so that the turkey couldn't see what was going to happen to it and run away. Yes, I know that the turkey was dead at this point, but it's traditional again. You then plucked any remaining feathers off it, pulled its giblets out and cooked it for many, many hours. If you started at four in the morning you were lucky if it was ready by bedtime. Of course freezing has done away with all this, and now you just spend all day waiting for the flippin' thing to defrost. But the ritual of studying, weighing and discussing the cooking time of the turkey still remains. As does the panicking about it being ready. I wonder if the turkey had any idea that he would have this much attention showered on him when he first arrived at the turkey farm. Perhaps this following diary, which I found inside an *Oven Ready Butter Basted*, might throw some light on the subject. I don't know who wrote it, or where they are now. Here it is:

TALKING TURKEY:
Monday

Well, we're finally off on our holidays. The farmer came out to see us off and our courier seemed so pleased to be driving us that he even gave the farmer some money! I know that this is going to be the trip of a lifetime! If I don't live past

the end of the week, I shall die happy. What am I saying – I've got years ahead of me yet. I'm not much more than a spring chicken. Well, autumn turkey anyway.

The journey itself was a bit boring, not to mention bumpy. You couldn't see a lot through the slats and some of the younger birds kept asking "Are we nearly there yet?" which got on my nerves slightly. But then somebody suggested a bit of a singsong, which really made things go with a swing. I joined in although I didn't know all the words. The chorus was easy though; it was gobble gobble gobble gobble gobble gobble gobble gobble gobble. It might sound a bit boring but it was fine with the tune. The journey then passed in no time.

When we got to our hotel there were the usual moans about the rooms. Yes, they were a bit cramped, but we weren't going to spend all our time in them, were we? And besides, the food more than made up for the rooms. There was plenty of it, in fact a bit too much. I tried to say as much to the waiter, but he didn't seem to understand. He just smiled and piled up my plate again. Must have thought it was Christmas!

Tuesday:

Went for a walk today; not too far. The camp Whitecoats wouldn't let us.

"Relax," they said. "You're not going anywhere."

They kept a very careful eye on us I must say. In fact, all the staff are very attentive. Nothing is too much trouble, especially if you want food. Met a very nice young "bird" from Norfolk. She's a bit on the plump side, but she seems very popular with the Whitecoats. They keep squeezing her and saying: "Oooh – Mr Mathews will like you!" I must confess it's making me quite jealous. But these holiday romances never go anywhere. Come the end of the week I doubt we'll ever see each other again.

Wednesday:

Went to the leisure centre with my "young lady" today. I'm not sure what her name is, but the Whitecoats call her Butterball – which could be a nickname, on account of her size. Bit personal if you ask me.

While I was there I thought I'd better weigh myself. Well, actually it wasn't really my idea – one of the Whitecoats just

popped me on the scales, but it was very thoughtful of him. You must watch your weight on holiday. Despite all the food I don't seem to have put on any weight, which pleased me no end, although Whitecoat – whose real name is Big Birds Ltd, according to his name tag – looked quite put out and immediately brought me a huge lunch. I tried to refuse but he was quite insistent. Oh well, my mother always said never bite the hand that feeds you, and you never know what's around the corner. So – party on!

Thursday:

Found a particularly attractive bit of grit, which I decided to present to my young lady as a sign of my affection.

After all, you have to grasp the nettle. Once you've made your mind up about something you should act. Life's too short to hang around. I had a spot of bother finding her. In fact, I couldn't track down most of our crowd actually, which is odd because they don't normally go off without saying anything. I was just about to give up hope of finding them, when I thought I'd give the leisure centre one last try. After all, we had been spending quite a bit of time in there; the Whitecoats encourage you to relax. They don't like to see you running around exerting yourself. Anyway, that's where I found her,

and frankly I wish I hadn't. Don't get me wrong, I'm as broad-minded as the next chap, and I realize that when you're on holiday things can go a bit further than normal, but this was too much. I looked through the window and there she was – bold as brass. And not just her; there was Owen Ready (I think that's his name, probably Welsh), with Giblets Inside and a number of our crowd. They were swinging on a trapeze type thing, some bit of gym equipment I suppose it was, without a care in the world, STARK NAKED! Yes! Not a stitch on! She must have seen me because she was hanging her head in shame, as well she might. She couldn't even look me in the eye. She just stared ahead as though I didn't exist. Well, that's it. I won't be talking to her ever again. She's only got herself to blame.

Friday:

Quite a few of the holidaymakers have left early. It's possible that they were only booked in for half a week, but I think it's far more likely that they were offended by the events of yesterday (you know – the nude trapeze act). Certainly I saw quite a few of them going to have a word with the manager in his office at a place called the Laughter House or something like that. I must confess I'm not too good at reading humish.

So – it's just me and the Skinny Brothers. The Whitecoats call them that. Very picky eaters, I must say. Still, all the more for me. And I am now beginning to stack the weight on, I'm ashamed to say, not that anyone else seems to mind. Oh well, I'm only here for a couple more days and then I'll soon work it off with a run. I'd go for one now but

I don't seem to be able to get out of my room. It's probably my imagination, but it seems to have got a lot smaller. And the door seems to have disappeared.

Saturday:

A couple of the Whitecoats are taking me for a drive. I wondered if the Skinny Brothers wanted to come but they didn't seem keen; oh well, it's their funeral. I've no idea where we're going. It's a bit of a mystery trip.

Later:

Well, no sooner had we got started than we pulled up at a restaurant. Honestly, do these Whitecoats ever think about anything other than food!

But no! I was wrong! We didn't go in for a meal, we went around to the kitchen. I thought that perhaps we were going to have a drink or something. I could certainly have done with one; this continual eating makes you very thirsty. But no! Wrong again! One of the Whitecoats put me on the floor, the man in the kitchen wearing a very silly tall white hat gave him some money and the Whitecoats left! Perhaps they are going for a meal after all. Well, I thought, I hope they remember where they've left me when it's time to go home! I can't say I was looking forward to sitting in a hot sweaty kitchen waiting for the Whitecoats. Silly Hat must have realized this because he started a game of chase. I was it. This was more like it! After almost a week of no exercise and stuffing my face I was ready for a good run. Try as he might, Silly Hat couldn't catch me.

Now it may have been the excitement of the moment, but Silly Hat spoilt the game for me by shouting and swearing. No matter how much fun you're having there's no call for that kind of language. Or throwing things. When a large knife whistled through my tail feathers I decided it was time to leave. He wouldn't see me for dust.

Sunday:

Running away when you don't know the area can be a very foolish thing. And frankly, although I have found a nice sheltered spot, and I certainly won't feel hungry for days, I am feeling rather lonely. But I had to get away from Silly Hat. Honestly, some people just can't play a simple game without resorting to bad sportsmanship.

Still, at least it's given me a chance to catch up on my diary. I'll just finish and then hide it in my special secret place, even if it does make it difficult to run.

Oh-oh, there's somebody coming. Oh, no, it's all right, it's just a farmer with his dog. How comforting he looks, strolling jauntily along with his trusty hound and walking stick. I must say I feel very safe knowing that he's seen me and is heading my way. He won't let anyone harm me. "Just let them try," I can almost hear him say, and they'd certainly get more than they bargained for, especially now that I can clearly see that his walking stick is a gun.

Oh. Considering where I found this diary, I've suddenly realized who our turkey is. Also considering where I found it I probably should have washed it before reading it!

Well, we've almost made it. Christmas Eve! This is possibly one of the most nerve-racking parts of Christmas, because you're just hours away from knowing whether all that hinting, cajoling and sucking up to parents has paid off. Time to reflect on the lengths you went to, to ensure a disappointment-free Christmas morning. And then shudder with embarrassment. You vow never to sink that low again; until next year.

Your little brother/sister/cousin (or perhaps all three) are hopping around as though someone has slipped a firecracker into their pants. You make a mental note that this is a good idea. Your mum is struggling to get them to bed:

"Father Christmas won't come if you don't go to bed," the adults all chorus. Of course, you realize the flaws in this argument. For a start, how will he *know* whether people are in bed or not? Does he land on the roof and then send an elf on ahead to check that everyone's asleep? Or does he slip down the chimney and take a chance? If this is the case, what happens if all the kids are still up watching the late night movie? Does he pop his head round the door and say: "Oh, sorry! I thought you were all in bed! I'll come back later, OK?" And that's another thing; if you go away for Christmas, how does he know where to deliver the presents? Does somebody tell him? The other thing that bothers me is this: what does Santa do if you're all *out*? Suppose you go to midnight mass at the local Church, and Santa calls before you get back. Does he think *Oh, they've probably gone to church*, or does he slip the presents under the front doormat and hope you don't step on them? Maybe he has an arrangement with your parents about where he should hide them. This seems unlikely; most parents can't even remember where they've put their own car keys, so the chances of them remembering something as complicated as where they've told Santa to hide the gifts is a total non-starter. Perhaps Santa has little cards that he slips under the doors of houses where he can't gain entry:

"Called at midnight but you were out. Parcels can be collected from the North Pole from Boxing Day onwards. Love, Santa. PS Please bring this card with you for easy identification."

The other big question is: How does Santa deliver everything at around midnight? Even allowing for the millions of children who can't tell the time, not to mention the millions of adults who can't work a clock, all of whom wouldn't realize if he was late, he stil must have a bit of a big job on.

I suppose time zones help. With Europe being an hour ahead of us, and bits of America being five or more hours behind I suppose it's just possible to get around the globe, but he'd have to step on it; and plan his route very carefully. Does he do that himself, or does he get the AA to work it out for him? That's probably the best way, because the AA would include road works (or rather no-fly zones), and enough Little Chefs to make sure that he didn't get too peckish en route.

These are probably just some of the thoughts that go through your head as you lie in bed, trying to get to sleep. Of course, it's not only the excitement of Christmas that's keeping you awake. In fact, it's probably not that at all. It's more likely to be the grunts and groans of the assorted relatives. Surely they don't make this amount of noise at home? If they do I'm amazed that the neighbours haven't petitioned to have them evicted. And then there's the cats – you're sleeping in the downstairs toilet, remember; *their* toilet. And one of them seems to have started Christmas early by eating something that has disagreed with it. A very easy thing to do at Christmas. You are just hours away from finding out whether or not your mum and dad bothered to read your "Dear Santa" letter, so ignore that cat and go to sleep.

But you can't.

You try but you're kept awake by grunting and groaning. Is this more relatives? No – it's something far more sinister. It's the sound of your parents. What are they up to? They're struggling to remove a bike that has been lodged in the back of the airing cupboard for three weeks.

Everyone had known it was there, even your little brother, who by an amazing coincidence had written to Santa asking for a bike. Several of you had even said: "What's that bike doing in the airing cupboard?" A question that your parents had fielded in the extra clever way that comes with being a parent:

"Stop being silly and eat your breakfast."

Amazingly it works; you stop asking. And when little brother unwraps the bike on Christmas morning he seems genuinely amazed, even though a pair of your dad's thermal underpants seem to have become inexplicably entwined in the bike chain.

Suspension of disbelief is one of the great magical mysteries of Christmas.

Now go to sleep.

Well, you made it! Of course it's four in the morning, you've had hardly any sleep due to trying to avoid the cats and various incontinent relatives, but you made it to THE BIG DAY.

Two thoughts race through your brain:

1. Have I got what I wanted?
2. Will I get through the day?

A quick inspection of the contents of your Santa Sack (AKA bin liner) reveals very little, particularly if the presents have been cleverly wrapped. Of course, sometimes they haven't. See if you can guess the contents of these parcels:

No matter how well you did in that little competition, it won't necessarily help you identify your own gifts. You'll just have to open them, and that's often the worst part. Imagine…

You're hoping for a personal stereo. You pick up a parcel. It is the right shape for a personal stereo. It's the right weight for one. But is it one?

Well, take the paper off and see.

No – it's a travel chess set, which by some cunningly clever award-winning design concept, turns into a travelling draughts set.[1]

"I thought you'd like that," says Dad, totally forgetting that it says "love from Santa" on the gift tag.

"Thanks, Dad."

If you've got any sense you'll force him to play it with you again and again and again as a punishment. Why do parents buy things like that? Do they imagine that, on the school bus next week you'll stand up and say:

"Anyone fancy a game of travel draughts?"

"Oooh, *yes please*!" choruses the entire bus.

The bus driver curses under his breath.

"Drat! If only I didn't have to drive this bus, I too could be having real fun playing draughts."

But still no personal stereo. You press on.

Pen refills for school. Wow!

A new school tie.

"Santa obviously knew that your other one was looking a bit frayed."

You make a mental note to find out who told him and take out a Mafia contract on them.

Open another gift. Could this be *the big one*?

No. New pants.

After unwrapping several things that loosely fall into

1: It's got a different set of holes on the back.

the category of *useful* (AKA boring), you're past caring. At this point you'd settle for anything that can't be used at school.

And it's at this point, as your finger is hooked under the fold of wrapping paper that will allow you access to the gift, that your parents say: "I think that's enough presents for the moment. Otherwise you'll have nothing to open later."

WHAT?!? You don't *care* about having nothing to open later; you want to open everything *NOW*. Get all the disappointment over in one hit.

But it is not to be. You're going to have to wait. Might as well see what everyone else has got.

Auntie Doreen went to midnight mass last night, and God has rewarded her (via Santa) with a set of exotic bath oils that are destined to cause an unsightly skin complaint that will have medical experts baffled for years; so it's not all bad news.

The lounge is now knee-deep in paper. Most of it, of course, has come from the presents for the younger children. Imagine what it will be like next year…

It hasn't escaped your notice that *their* presents are much bigger and more interesting than yours. Of course, the *size* of the package shouldn't be important; just because the package is small, that doesn't mean that the contents are boring; the one thing doesn't follow the other. Except at Christmas. Oh well, there's still more things to open later. Right now it's time to play Hunt the Cousin. One of the smaller cousins has disappeared under the mass of Christmas paper and is currently being searched for.

Some of the wrapping has already been taken out to the bin.

"Perhaps he's been taken out with it," you suggest, with just a bit too much hope in your voice.

"Don't be silly!" says your mum, and immediately goes into the garden to rifle through the rubbish. Not there.

He finally turns up inside the box of one of his presents. He will now spend the entire day playing in this box, which he is much more excited about than any of the extremely amazing and expensive presents that his parents and relatives queued for hours to buy him. Sorry - wrote to Santa for.

"We should just get him a box next year!" the adults joke. *Put him in a box and send him to someone you really hate*, you think but don't say.

After all, this is Christmas; a time for families to get together and communicate. You haven't seen each other since last Christmas. There is so much to talk about.

You put the telly on.

"Don't put the telly on," your mother complains. "It's Christmas. Let's have a conversation."

The novelty value of this suggestion seems to appeal to everyone, and in the spirit of good will to all persons, you all have a conversation; about what to watch on telly. This develops into an argument and results in most of you not talking all morning. But the telly stays off.

It's a pity because there's lots to choose from on the telly. *Chitty Chitty Bang Bang* and *James Bond* are on a bit later.

And the soaps have really pulled the stops out to reflect the festive spirit:

One of them has got a multiple pile-up that kills half of the cast, another has an outbreak of a deadly killer virus, and Coronation Street has some blokes talking in a pub.

Just when you think it can't get any worse, someone says:

"Let's play charades!"

They must have a death wish.

Amazingly, everyone agrees. At least, they agree to play. What they can't seem to find any common ground on is what the various hand movements mean.

"Is a book the one where you mime curtains?"

"NO! You have to tug your ear!"

"That's *sounds like*."

"No. That's when you put two fingers on your forearm."

"Why don't we just *play*?" suggests your dad, without realizing that unless you establish the basic format the whole thing will be a disaster. Just play; the whole thing will be a disaster anyway. Your sister, who seems to have hit on a totally new way to play, spends the entire game saying:

"My go! I'm going to do *The Lion King*!"

Despite this announcement, and the fact that she puts on the *Lion King* playsuit that she got for last Christmas, then performs a mime that Marcelle Marceau would be proud of, most of your relatives struggle and fail to identify the film.

"Is it *The Italian Job*?"

You sit with a fixed grin, hoping for the ground to open up and swallow you whole. It doesn't. It's your own fault. If you'd thought to put that on your Santa list, it might have done.

"Dear Santa – can you fix it for me so that if anyone suggests playing charades the ground opens up and swallows me whole? Thank you."

This is a good time to slip away from the *excitement* and study the next section of this book. Without it things may just continue downhill. In all fairness they'll probably continue downhill anyway, but at least you'll be able to cope.

Getting away from a "family having fun" is not as easy as it seems. They'll resent you leaving. After all, if they're forced to stay and enjoy themselves, why shouldn't you be? So, grab one of the cardboard boxes that your little brother/sister/cousin's toy came in, and using the scissors from the Barbie Fashion Set that one of them is bound to have had, cut out a life-sized image of yourself. Add a few details using the obligatory Christmas felt pen set. Very little detail will be necessary, because most of your relatives have lost track of what you look like anyway. Having done this, prop the cut-out on the sofa and inch slowly out of the room.

Having found a quiet corner where you won't be disturbed – the attic is probably your only hope – study the following A-Z survival guide.

ACCEPTING GIFTS

It's possible – no, sorry, inevitable – that some of the things you get for Christmas won't be to your liking. In fact, you'll hate them. But if you want as stress-free a Christmas as possible it won't do to show it, as the gift will almost certainly be from a relative.

A WHOLE BUCKET OF MANURE, YOU SHOULDN'T HAVE...

YOU CAN KEEP THE BUCKET AS WELL

COPING:

You'll need to prepare your face so that disappointment can't creep over it without you knowing. Take your time opening the gift, and accompany this with lots of "I wonder what it can possibly be" acting. As the last bit of paper comes off, without looking at the gift say: "Wow! Thanks! I'll have a really good look at that later." and put it to one side. If you remember, but it doesn't matter if you don't, it can be a good idea later on to say: "I had a chance to really look at your gift whilst you were throwing up in the toilet. It's great!" Behold one happy – if nauseous – relative.

BRANDY

A family Christmas dinner can go on for ever. Because you don't have a stomach the size of an industrial dustbin, you'll probably find that you are full fairly early on. Unfortunately, your parents will almost certainly make you stay at the table, because they think it's not polite to leave while other people are still shovelling nosh like they've never seen any before.

COPING:

Offer to pour brandy over the Christmas pudding. If your parents say: "Don't be silly!" explain that this is traditional; older relatives will back you up. Away from the table pour as much brandy over the pudding as possible. The idea then is that someone else sets fire to it, once you've excused yourself and popped out of the room for a minute.

"Just going to the loo – won't be a minute. Carry on without me."

You hear the match being struck even as you close the door.

This should clear the table pretty fast, and the arrival of the fire brigade just might add a bit of necessary excitement to an otherwise dull day.[1]

1: Obviously I'm not *seriously* suggesting you do this!

COLOURFUL SWEATERS

These are one of those terrible Christmas presents that seem to crop up every year, usually bought or – worse still – *made* – by a relative. I had an aunt who was obsessed with knitting. Give her two sticks and a ball of wool and she was away. It didn't even have to be wool. We once had a Chinese take-away and I made the mistake of giving her chopsticks. Within seconds the walls were covered in flying bits of Chinese food and she'd turned the noodles into a sweet 'n' sour bobble hat. If a relative knits you a sweater for Christmas, watch out – you'll be forced to wear it all day.

COPING:

Sneak the TV remote out of the room and hide it up your new jumper. Then go back into the room where everyone is watching the big Christmas blockbuster (AKA *Chitty Chitty Bang Bang*) and – through your jumper – keep changing the channels.

"Who's doing that?" the room will chorus.

"Erm … I think it's this sweater. The pattern is so strong that it's interfering with the TV signal." You can demonstrate, although this probably won't be necessary; TV is some form of witchcraft as far as most adults are concerned.

"You'd better take it off then!"

Sorted!

DOGS

As you know, dogs can be nasty, smelly, stupid things, which is probably why people accept them so readily as a part of the family. Dogs love this and try and muscle in at every opportunity. Christmas seems to bring out the worst in them, probably because relatives spoil them. You find them (dogs, not relatives!) leaping all over you.

COPING:

Actually, this can come in handy at Christmas. Apart from being a useful place to put unwanted food, dogs will readily take the blame for almost anything that happens: spilt drinks, broken toys, strange smells. Keep the dog with you at all times on Christmas day; you really don't need any more hassle than normal.

A WORD OF WARNING:
DON'T LET THIS NEW CLOSE FRIENDSHIP SPREAD BEYOND THE CHRISTMAS PERIOD. DOGS ARE AMAZINGLY LOYAL, AND YOU'LL FIND THAT YOU SIMPLY CAN'T GET RID OF THEM!

ENERGY

This is something you're going to need a lot of over Christmas, particularly if you want to stay ahead of the game and out of trouble.

COPING:

Pace yourself. If you find this too difficult then wait until all of the relatives are asleep – this is bound to happen after lunch – and move all of their watches forward a few hours. When they wake up they're bound to check the time.

"Oh gosh! It's bed time!" they'll say, and take themselves off upstairs, leaving you with the house to yourself. With any luck, they'll take any small children with them!

FASHION

This is something that parents and older relatives know absolutely nothing about. Unfortunately they think they do. Consequently when they're thinking of what to get you for Christmas, clothes are a definite possibility. Clothes that *they* think are fashionable.

COPING:

If you get even the slightest inkling that a grown-up is thinking of buying you clothes, try and persuade them to give you money instead.

"Oh, you don't want money! It's boring." They might say. Let them know that you think money is brilliant. Tell them that you're saving up for something, but DO NOT tell them that it's clothes. If you do they'll say:

"Good idea! You could do with some new school shoes," and they won't shut up about it until you buy some!

GIFT TOKENS

Unfortunately if you say the word *money*, some adults think you mean *gift token*. Gift tokens are OK – better than nothing (almost) – but try using them and you'll find that they just don't have the same flexible spending power that cash has.

COPING:

Spend a bit of time encouraging a younger brother/sister that they really want a particular thing that they have forgotten to ask Santa for; this is because they didn't realize that they wanted it. This will unfortunately involve talking to them quite a bit, but it'll be worth it and you'll soon recover. Make sure that whatever it is you are persuading the small child that they want to buy can be bought with a gift token, otherwise the whole thing is a waste of time. Having really wound them up, offer to swap any gift tokens you get for any cash they get.[1] Get them to swear to it. Writing it in their blood can be surprisingly satisfying!

1: Try to negotiate a favourable exchange rate, i.e. a £5 gift token for £10 cash. Pick a child who does not understand money.

Then all you have to do is move in fast after they get their cash and before they change their mind.

HOME MOVIES

There is something – a death wish probably – that makes parents and older relatives very keen to make home movies of everything. And they seem to get decidedly worse at Christmas. They shoot footage of the present opening, the eating, the drinking, the game playing, Her Majesty – everything. As they move around the room, trying to look and act as much like a geriatric Steven Spielberg as possible, your mind fast-forwards to the time when they show this film and attempt to recapture the moment. Agh!

COPING:

You are also capable of working a video camera, remember. After all, if an adult can do it it's got to be very easy. You are also probably capable of being far more creative than they are – and sneaky. One of the great features of a family Christmas is the fact that families talk about each other behind their backs. This often explains why parents and so on often go quiet as you enter the room; they don't want you knowing that they've just been slagging off your auntie:

Don't interrupt these family discussions – video them; on the same tape as the present unwrapping, etc.

When the moment comes for the family to gather for the Premier Gala performance of "The Wilsons – Xmas 1999" just sit back and wait; you won't be disappointed!

A WORD OF CAUTION:
Make sure nobody gets their hands on the video camera and does it to you!

INVITATIONS

I don't know exactly why, although it's probably due to the Christmas spirit of Good Will to All Men (and Women), but your parents usually decide to invite the neighbours round for pre- or post-Christmas drinks and nibbles (AKA cheap plonk and Twiglets). This is a problem because many of the neighbours can't stand each other. It's usually an even bigger problem for you because you can't stand any of them.

COPING:

Your parents will spend hours and hours carefully working out who to invite and when, so that the various neighbours that can't abide each other don't get invited on the same night. You should offer a bit of advice:

"Why don't you get some little invitation cards. Make it look a bit special."

Your parents will jump at this; all adults like a chance to show off. You then volunteer your younger brother/sister to put the cards into envelopes and deliver them – you may have to bribe/threaten them to go along with this. All you have to do is make sure that little brother/sister puts the wrong card in the wrong envelope; this shouldn't be difficult as they always walk around with their shoes on the wrong feet. You should then arrange to be out on the various nights of the various drinks parties, unless of course you like the sight of blood.

JANUARY SALES

You are almost certainly going to get something for Christmas that you really don't want. Having done the acceptance speech as described earlier, you probably feel as though you're now stuck with it for life, or at least until you can arrange for the dog to have an accident with it.

COPING:

Don't worry. The January sales have been set up precisely to help in this situation. Most stores take goods back without receipts and without giving you the third degree. You just have to go in and say "This doesn't work," and they give you a new one. It's also quite easy to exchange something you don't want for something you do, as long as they are similar things, and cost roughly the same amount of money.

"This radio cassette recorder doesn't work. I'd rather have a personal stereo anyway."

That would probably work.

"These socks are hideous. I'd rather have a 24-inch TV with Nicam stereo anyway."

That probably wouldn't, but don't let that stop you trying!

KISSING

Many relatives are obsessed with trying to kiss you. I don't know why, maybe they don't get out much or simply can't find anyone fool enough to snog them. Anyway it can be a real pain.

COPING:

All you need are a few Rice Crispies, a small tube of glue and some modelling paint. Glue the crispies to a small area of one cheek; small enough for you to be able to cover it with your hand. After all, you don't want your parents seeing it and sending you to bed for the day. Use the modelling paint to make the crispies look festering and infectious. Now you're ready. The unsuspecting relative will approach saying:

"Come here and give your old granny a kiss!"

Willingly offer them your cheek. As they recoil, say: "It's OK. I'm not *very* infectious!"

The crispies should last for a while. (You weren't planning on washing over Christmas, were you?) If you're lucky they might even start spreading.

LAUGH-I THOUGHT I'D NEVER START

One of the great sources of amusement at Christmas is the cracker joke. Supposedly. In fact, they're really torturous.

COPING:

You can actually get more fun out of watching people trying to make them funny, and seeing the lengths they go to to explain them if you appear not to understand. One way to achieve this is to open the crackers up and memorize all the punch lines to the jokes (not that difficult). You then carefully reseal them and wait for cracker-joke-telling time. This usually happens over Christmas dinner.

THEM: "Why is Brazilian honey so difficult to come by ?"

YOU: "Because there's only one bee in Brazil."

THEM: "Yes!"

YOU: "So?"

THEM: "It's funny."

YOU: "Not if you really like honey, it isn't."

THEM: "No! It's not a bee..."

YOU: "Then why does it say that then?"

THEM: " No! It's a play on words – look – they don't mean bee."

They show you the joke. By now they're starting to get exasperated.

YOU: "Yes they do. They've just spelt it wrong. It's probably a printing error."

By now other people are joining in. Your big brother/sister who's just home from university and thinks they're SOO COOOL has a go. Steam is coming out of the ears of the person who originally started the joke and is now wishing that they hadn't.

YOU: "Maybe the climate in Brazil isn't suitable for bee-keeping, or..."

We hear the sound of somebody's head exploding. Bits of brain land on Uncle Frank's plate.

"No thanks. I couldn't eat another thing."

MINE!

One of the many sources of argument over Christmas is who do the contents of a cracker belong to? The person whose plate the cracker was next to at the start of the meal? Or the person holding on to the main part of the cracker once the thing has been pulled? You might think that the fairest way would be for everyone to have whatever comes out of the cracker on to their plate, but this doesn't always work out, because often the stuff in somebody else's cracker is much better than the stuff in yours. And that's when the fights break out.

COPING:

Get to the crackers before Christmas and pull them open slightly so that you can see what is inside them. Check their weight so that you get to recognize the contents just by shaking the cracker. Then insert a rubber band up through the cracker, attaching it at each end in a way that it's not visible.

Having done that, put the crackers back in their box ready for Christmas. When it comes to cracker pulling time, establish a house rule that whoever gets the main bit of the cracker gets to keep the toy/novelty/whatever from inside. Then, each time you pull a cracker with somebody else, give it a little shake first:

"Just making sure there's something inside," you explain, although you're actually identifying the contents. You can then decide whether you want them or not. If you do, you simply keep a tight hold on the cracker as you pull it. Because of the rubber band, after the bang the whole thing will come to you, including the contents.

If you don't want it you simply let the cracker go and the entire thing will spring over to the other person, possibly hitting them on the nose, which could be a bonus. They'll be delighted to have won, and ignore the blood. They'll also ignore the rubber band, which they will assume has come off the hat! Brilliant!

NUTS

One of the most irritating things at Christmas is the relative who keeps cracking nuts. Imagine that you're settled in front a great film – yes, I appreciate that the words "great film" and "Christmas" don't normally go together, but imagine for once that they do. Every time there's a really good bit – *CRACK* – another nut bites the dust. It is really starting to drive you mad. Walnuts are the worst. They take ages to crack, and when finally they do break, bits fly all around the room, up your nose, down your socks etc. It's really annoying.

But it can be avoided.

COPING:

Get hold of the walnuts before anyone else does and carefully prise them open with a penknife. Remove the nut and then glue the two bits of shell back together again. Not only will they crack a lot easier, but the fact that they are all empty should cause the irritating relative to give up. Of course, it may not – in which case you'll need plan B, which is...

Open the nut by the same method and put a little note inside one, which reads: "Leave us nuts alone, or the Big Cracker will get you." That should sort them out!

OH

As I said earlier, hiding your disappointment at Christmas can be difficult. Impossible even.

COPING:

Practise saying the word "oh". It's a useful word and can be employed in a hundred different Christmas situations. For instance: When you open a gift that you absolutely *hate* but want to appear to like: "OH!"

It's noncommittal and means that you don't have to say anything else; the person who gave you the gift will interpret it in their own favour anyway.

It can also be used to show polite disapproval.

"Let's watch *Chitty Chitty Bang Bang*."

"Oh."

"Unless you'd rather watch something else."

"Well, Lawnmower Death are live in concert on Channel 4."

Anything's better than *Chitty Chitty Bang Bang*. Almost.

Experiment with the word "oh". You'll find that it fits any situation.

PARTY GAMES

There may be a time over Christmas when somebody will suggest playing party games; if the TV blows up, for instance. Although these can be quite fun to watch, they can be humiliating to take part in; particularly where relatives are concerned. The most humiliating is charades.

COPING:

When it comes to your turn, pick a film so obscure or impossible to mime that you get yourself disqualified. This a good one:

The Persecution of Jean-Paul Marat as performed by the inmates of the Asylum of Charenton under the direction of the Marquis de Sade.

Just in case you get accused of making it up you can show off by saying that it was made in 1966 in Delux colour, was 116 minutes long (slightly shorter than the title) and starred Glenda Jackson. They'll have heard of her; she's now a Member of Parliament.

QUEEN'S SPEECH

As I mentioned earlier, the Queen makes a speech to the nation on Christmas day. She tells us about all the wonderful stuff she's been doing and reminds us about all the naughty things that we *shouldn't* be doing. It's probably the only time of year that she's allowed to tell us off. After all, she's not really in charge, is she? But lots of people insist on watching her. I'm not sure whether this is because they're hoping that she'll say something interesting, or whether it's because they think she'll have their heads chopped off if they don't. Either way, if you're in a household that insists on watching the Queen's speech, you'll be forced to watch it too.

COPING:

Well, actually it only lasts about 15 minutes, but if you really can't handle it then this might be a good opportunity to slip into your new jumper again, just to check if it's still affecting the TV reception.

"Yes. It is. Sorry about that!"

"Get out! And take that jumper with you!"

REST

As I also said earlier you'll need a lot of energy to get through Christmas. You'll have got up, or been woken up, very early, and you'll be called upon to do all sorts of jobs, quite apart from having to entertain difficult relatives. Rest is something you'll be very lucky to get any of, because even when the relatives crash out after lunch, it'll probably be your job to keep an eye on your little brothers/sisters/cousins, and make sure the animals don't eat the turkey etc.

COPING:

Inform everyone that you've set up a murder mystery.

"Clues," you tell them, "are hidden all over the house."

"Wow! That sounds fun!" they'll all chorus and set

off to solve the mystery. You can then put your feet up and relax, play with your new Christmas presents etc. Or sleep. They won't bother you for hours. Why? Because they'll be too busy searching for clues. And why are the clues so hard to find? Because they don't exist!

SPROUTS

Christmas is full of strange things that don't really happen at any other time of the year. One of these strange phenomena is *sprouts*. They're available all year round, and some people eat them all year round, but they really come into their own at Christmas. They are as much a part of the Christmas experience as getting a gift you don't want or forgetting a gift for the one person you really like. Either way, you are going to find a great pile of sprouts on your plate whether you like them or not. If you like them, no problem; but you probably don't.

THE DOG LOVES BRUSSELS SPROUTS

THINK AGAIN!

COPING:

All you need are a few cocktail sticks. There's bound to be some around, because at this time of year adults always want strange things in their drinks: cherries, pickled onions, small bits of liver, etc. And all of these need to be on a stick (especially the liver). Take a few sticks and join the sprouts together with them, so that they form the shape of a very small man; or woman. Actually it's more likely to be unisex, unless you're extremely creative with your sprouts. Having done this you suddenly throw up your hands in horror and say:

"Look! My dinner's being attacked by Martians!"

The "Martian" (AKA Little Sprout Person) will be removed immediately and thrown in the bin. There are a few risks attached to this particular ploy: your parents may not believe that this is an actual Martian. In which case the worst you'll get is a telling off for playing with your food.[1]

The big problem I suppose is if your grannie turns out to be an X-Files fan. Before you can stop her and explain that it was a joke she'll be on the phone to Mulder and Sculley, or - even worse - the local paper. Your little sprout Martian could make the front page of the *Daily Star*, and then everyone will believe that it's true.

You may be thinking: "Oh come on! Nobody would think that a few sprouts held together with cocktail sticks was a Martian!" In which case - read on.

1: Unless your actions cause one or more of your frailer relatives to have a fatal heart attack, in which case you might get sent to your room.

TIPPLE

Just as Christmas is a time when people eat far too much and far too many strange things, so it's also a time when people drink too much as well. People who normally don't have anything stronger than spring water with a hint of apple find themselves buying and consuming all sorts of strange beverages.

"Would you like a drink?"

"Yes, please. Have you got a purple one?"

They don't care what it is, they just throw it down their necks.

"After all, it's Christmas. We should be enjoying ourselves!" says Mum as she downs a pint of egg-nog and sets fire to the kitchen.

COPING:

There's nothing wrong with anyone having a little tipple at Christmas, although it's obviously boring for you if you're the only one left standing; you'll have to keep an eye on the *kids*, for a start. But apart from that, it's not too bad. After all, most adults will fall asleep after a couple of glasses of wine, especially on Christmas Day, and that gives you control of the TV. You can watch whatever you want; you can even turn it off, because there's probably not anything worth watching. The snoring is another matter!

Of course if the drinking really annoys you, you can wait until they've all had a few and then show them your sprout Martian. They'll all vow never to touch another drop (until next year!).

UNWANTED VISITORS

Some people, usually people that nobody likes, seem to make a habit of dropping in on neighbours on Christmas Day. Maybe they've forgotten to buy their own Christmas dinner and they're hoping to share yours. Or perhaps they just like annoying people. Who knows? Whatever the reason, it's the last thing you want on top of a lot of relatives, because you can bet that your parents will tell you to amuse these people until they finish whatever they're doing. Of course they aren't really doing anything, and they never finish it. It's just a ruse to get out of talking to neighbours. Unfortunately, the problem is then dumped on you.

ER...NOW KATIE WILL PLAY HER RECORDER

COPING:

The doorbell goes. You can tell that it's unwanted visitors because they'll try and make the doorbell sound like a cheery Christmas tune; or they may even sing a few snatches of a carol; badly of course.

"I'll go," you say to Mum and Dad before they can tell you to. As you leave the kitchen to go to the front door, grab the turkey giblets and place them on your head. Open the front door and say:

141

"Hello! Come in! We've just had a bit of an accident with the turkey!"

This will almost certainly cause your visitors to say:

"It's OK – we'll come back another time. Merry Christmas!" Because they'll assume that something even more sinister is going on; some strange black magic ritual or something. Whatever they think you're unlikely to see them again over Christmas – or ever!

VISITING

The one thing worse than having relatives visiting you at Christmas is visiting them. At least in your own home you can disappear for a bit.

"Sorry, I just went to look for something and I accidentally locked myself in the attic."

But if you're in somebody else's house you can't really do that. You could try I suppose, but it probably wouldn't work. No, you have to sit there being on your best behaviour. At dinner you can't even help yourself to seconds, although you'll probably have trouble managing *firsts*.

COPING:

Sit very still and look confused. If the relative whose house it is speaks to you, answer very politely but don't be familiar in any way. Your parents will be surprised by this, but they won't stop you because they'll be delighted that you're being so polite. But why are you doing it? Well, what you're trying to do is make your relative think that they've accidentally invited the wrong family by mistake. After an initial embarrassment they'll be only too glad to get rid of you. Let's face it, nobody can take your parents in anything more than a very small dose.

"Well, it's been lovely seeing you. Goodbye," the confused relative will say. Your parents will think they've outstayed their welcome, leave and make a mental note not to go back next year.

WIND

I don't want to make too much of this, but it's a known medical fact that too much rich food and drink (and sprouts) can cause … er … digestion problems. In fact, this can get so bad that it's possible to fly a kite indoors. You'd think that because of this, a kite would make the ideal Christmas present, but no.

Anyway, this problem gets worse the older you get. Which means that you probably won't be suffering personally, but you will be suffering the effects – if you follow me.

COPING:

One of the Christmas presents that parents often get, that nobody can quite see the point of, is candles. But I'm about to explain their purpose. What you do is this: you gather all the candles you can find and bring them into whichever room is the windiest. You then say: "Let's light these Christmas candles. They'll look lovely."

No one will argue with this, because they *will* look lovely. They'll also have the desired effect, because:

a) They are perfumed.

b) They are naked flames.

Anyone with even the most basic knowledge of science will know that certain things are highly flammable, especially when exposed to a naked flame. Certain gases fall into this category. It would not be a good idea to expose them to a naked flame. And you have just filled the room with ... yes, you guessed it ... naked flames.

I think you'll enjoy the sight of a number of relatives clenching everything and trying to prevent a large explosion. I know I would.

XYLOPHONE

Parents can always be relied upon, when they're inviting relatives for Christmas, to invite the one child in the family who is noisy, nasty and determined to make everybody else's Christmas hell. As it screams, demands and stamps its feet you wonder how you are possibly going to be able to put up with this for the next week or so. But don't worry – help is at hand.

COPING:

Make sure this child is on your Christmas list. Beg steal or borrow enough money to buy it a present: a xylophone; or a drum; or anything really noisy. (A xylophone is as noisy as but more subtle than a drum.) The child will love it. He or she will want to play it non-stop. You may find this unbearable, but I can assure you that adults won't be able to put up with it for as long as you can. Adults are a lot less laid back and tolerant than you are, as I'm sure you've noticed. In almost no time at all, your parents will be trying to take the xylophone/drum/very noisy thing off the child. When this fails the child will be banished to another room. Better still an argument will break out, causing the child and its parents to go off in a huff, never to return.

YOU

In the mad hurly-burly that is Christmas Day you may feel that one person gets forgotten. Namely – YOU. Once you've been given your presents your parents will be getting on with their own Christmas quite probably; either that or they'll be entertaining visitors and relatives, panicking about turkeys or whether or not there's enough tonic water and so on. They'll ignore you completely.

COPING:

Disguise yourself as a complete stranger and knock on the front door. Without you to get rid of unwanted guests, your parents will be forced to let you in.

HI, I'M A COMPLETE STRANGER, MUM

They'll probably even invite you to stay for lunch:

"You can sit in [your name]'s place. I don't know where they've disappeared to. Still, that's their look-out!" [1]

As you settle down to enjoy Christmas dinner, you'll find that they lavish attention on you. You'll even be allowed to refuse certain foods:

"No Brussels sprouts for me thanks, they're completely disgusting."

"Would you like to watch *Chitty Chitty Bang Bang* later?"

"Do I look demented?"

If you're really lucky they'll dig out a Christmas present for you. But don't get too excited, it's bound to be socks!

1: This is a mark of how little regard your parents have for you. You go missing on Christmas Day, but do they look for you? Of course not. They'd rather entertain a complete stranger, even if it is you in disguise!

ZOO

Home at Christmas time can feel a bit like a madhouse. What am I saying – it IS a madhouse.

COPING:

Go to the zoo. You'll find it far more civilized.

EXCUSE ME, COULD YOU PASS THE ZEBRA, PLEASE?

Well, I hope you found that useful.

At the very least it will have kept you away from the bosom of your family for a while. And if you've read this really slowly, Christmas Day might even be over. Time to crawl into bed with the cats and their litter-tray. Oh well, that's Christmas finished for another year.

BOXING DAY:

No, it isn't! There's plenty more where that came from! There's still two thirds of a turkey to get through yet.

"Are the shops open?" asks Gorgeous Cousin.

What?!?

You'd almost forgotten about him/her. But then you've had your hands full; though not full of Gorgeous Cousin unfortunately. Full of trying to get through a family Christmas without going completely mental.

The rest of the family have already sussed that the shops *are* open. Boxing Day used to be the day when you gave small gifts (Christmas Boxes) to the servants; now it's the day when you put your unwanted gifts *back* in their box and take them to be exchanged at the shops.[1]

Using walking the dog as an excuse, one by one the relatives slip out of the house. The dog is over the moon. So are you; considering the amount of sprouts you fed him yesterday it's not safe for him to be in a confined space. A few hours later, everyone gathers for lunch. The dog is sprawled on the carpet, daring anyone to suggest anything that involves movement.

1: Although you can wait for the January sales, when you'll get a better deal.

"Wasn't that sweater green earlier, Frank?" your mum enquires of Uncle Frank, knowing that it was, because she bought it.

"Oh, I don't think so," lies Frank.

"Must have been a trick of the light, then."

Let's hope they don't notice you.

"Wasn't that 24-inch Nicam Stereo TV set a pair of socks earlier?"

There are several options on Boxing Day. You can carry on where you left off the day before: eating, sleeping, eating, sleeping and so on, or you can have a change: sleep, eat, sleep, eat, sleep, eat and so on. Or you can go to the pantomime.

"Goody!" chorus the younger children. "We're going to the pantomime!"

As an actor I have to say that one of the cruellest things you can do is go to the pantomime on Boxing Day. Most of the cast have had one day off for Christmas – Christmas Day strangely enough. They've had far too much to eat and drink, and they've also had far too many problems getting from home at the other end of the country back to the theatre where they're appearing in panto. This is due to the lack of a decent train service on Boxing Day.[1]

"We apologize for the late running of this service. This is due to an actor on the train."

The last thing the actors want to do after all this is act. The last thing the grown-ups want to do is *watch* them acting. And the first thing the children want to do is run around and make as much noise as possible. Can you blame them? They spent the whole of the previous day stuck indoors being nice to relatives.

But at least the panto provides a fitting end to another Christmas. The cast take their bows in all their finery, then the Good Fairy steps forward:

AND NOW OUR SHOW IS OVER,
WE HOPE YOU'VE ALL HAD FUN,
CHRISTMAS IS ALSO OVER NOW,
BUT THERE'LL BE ANOTHER ONE.

What's she on about – over now? There's another TEN days yet!

1: There's never a decent train service – there's no reason why Boxing Day should be any different.

A PARTRIDGE IN A PEAR TREE

"Sorry, I couldn't eat another thing."

No! On the first day of Christmas my true love gave to me a partridge in a pear tree. The big question I suppose is, why? And what about the two turtle doves somebody left on the step on Boxing Day?

But the fact remains that there are still another TEN days of Christmas. Christmas Day is just the start of it. Christmas lasts all the way through to Epiphany, on 6 January.

Excuse me there's somebody at the door.

No. Nobody. Just three French hens. Oh well, I was out of cat food.

Anyway – you have to make sure the decorations are down by Twelfth Night (5 January), or you'll have a year of bad luck. Excuse me: the door again.

What am I supposed to do with four calling birds? I don't even know what calling birds *are*, let alone what you do with them. Was that the phone?

Five rings. And when I got there they'd rung off. This is all getting rather sinister.

Anyway – where were we? Twelfth Night. Yes … excuse me. Door.

Do any of you like goose eggs? I've got six of them. And seven swans.

Not to mention eight maids a' milking, nine ladies

dancing, ten lords a' leaping, eleven pipers piping and twelve drummers drumming.

And I was worried about only getting socks for Christmas. Now the house is packed!

This is ridiculous! I've only just got rid of a house full of relatives. Besides, what are the neighbours going to say? You can imagine the racket. And the smell. It's almost worse than Uncle Frank!

I can't stand it, I'm just going to leave them to it. Just a minute:

"Listen, you lot! Excuse me! Could you stop dancing and leaping for a minute and listen! Ouch! Can you keep that partridge under control, please? I've got to nip out for a bit (a week actually but don't tell *them* that!) – there's plenty of mince pies in the cupboard and if you get really peckish there's loads of turkey. Ooops!"

That was not quite the right thing to say in a room full of poultry. I think I'll nip round to Mrs. Wibley's. She's having a few odd friends round for drinks. If I know anything about *her* friends they'll be *very* odd.

And so, with the geese snapping at the flapping legs of my corduroy flares – a Christmas present in case you didn't guess – I head for the door.

I may have put Christmas Day behind me. I may even have avoided the worst excesses of Boxing Day. But it's still not over. What about New Year's Eve? How am I going to keep awake until 12 o'clock? How am I going to stop my mother playing the bagpipes, which she insists on doing every year?

"It's traditional," she tells me.

"It's traditional in Scotland. It's also traditional to have them played *properly*."

Oh well, I'll soon be among friends at Mrs Wibley's. I'm not going empty handed; I'm taking seven tins of ravioli that I've got left over from the hamper.

AFTERWORD

You may be wondering why I didn't invite my usual team of experts to help me research and write this book. There are a couple of reasons for this:

1. I wanted to go it alone, thus avoiding unnecessary expense (i.e. paying them!).
2. I wanted the book to reflect a normal Christmas, and – let's face it – none of my hand-picked team could be described as *normal*!

Coping
with

If you thought *Coping with Christmas* was tough, let's see how you get to grips with these...

Coping with School
Why do you need to bother with homework? What really goes into school dinners? Smuggle this book into class and find out the answers.

Coping with Teachers
How can you tell if your teacher is an alien? Prepare to be shocked and amazed as Peter Corey uncovers the truth about this strange species.

Coping with Parents
Do you have one or more parents? And do you find them a problem? Don't worry – you're not alone and here's your chance to hit back!

Coping with Friends
Bossy friends, mad friends, clubs, gangs and secret societies – Peter Corey covers them all.

Coping with the Family
Large or small, love it or hate it,
almost everybody has one – a family,
that is. Find out how to cope and family
life will never be the same again.

Coping with Pets
Eye-opening advice on all our furry,
scaly, feathered and slimy friends.

Coping with Boys/Girls
A flip book that helps you put the
opposite sex in their place!

Coping with Love
Blissed out or ready to puke? If you
think love is a pain in the neck, then
this book will help you cope.

Coping with Exams and Tests
Swot up on tried and tested cheating methods,
revision timetables and how to cope with
the F-word – FAILURE!

Coping with the 21st Century
Find out what the future holds and
whether or not you'll like it!